The
Who, What, When, Where, Why, and How
of Baseball

Revised & Updated Edition

The
Who, What, When, Where, Why, and How
of Baseball

Revised & Updated Edition

by
Jim Charlton

BARNES
&NOBLE
BOOKS
NEW YORK

1999 Barnes & Noble Books

ISBN 1-56619-070-3

Illustrations copyright © 1990 by Michael A. Schacht

Interior design and typography by Noble Desktop Publishers

Printed and bound in the United States of America

00 01 02 03 M 9 8 7 6 5 4

BVG

Contents

Introduction

Baseball, as every fan knows, is steeped in history, each season connecting inextricably with those in the past. This thread exists in other sports as well, but just barely. Baseball more than any other spectator sport looks to what has gone before. Hockey fans honor the past, at least to the extent of recognizing the years their team last won the Stanley Cup, followers of football barely acknowledge the game as it was before the Super Bowl, and pro basketball is strictly contemporary. In the NBA, anything before 1980 is ancient history, something to do with peach baskets and center jumps.

Baseball is the marvelous interweaving of players, statistics and pennant winners that joins one generation to the next. We compare averages and records between stars of different decades, argue the pitching motions and batting stances of players who toiled half a century apart. Thanks to computers, pennant winning teams from one era can now face off against a team from a different time. Generally speaking, careers last longer in baseball than other sports so we become familiar and comfortable with ball players. We can grow up with them or grow old watching them play. It is easy for a fan to draw a nexus, say, between the handful of Red Sox left fielders spanning an amazing seven decades. Williams, Yastrzemski, Rice, and Greenwell, just four players at one position in all those years. A rich legacy that certainly has no equal in other sports.

For me, this relationship was underscored again while researching and writing the revised edition of this book. Discussing Rickey Henderson, for instance, leads to Harry Hooper; Hooper is tied to Speaker, Speaker to Cobb, and Cobb back to Henderson. It all comes around in a circle. The meandering quality of the answers in the book—yes, and a few of the questions tend to ramble also—is appealing to a writer, and I hope to the reader. It allowed me to discuss a situation or game or player more fully than a typical Q and A book might have. For that, I thank my publisher.

There are others I would like to thank as well. The Society of American Baseball Researchers (SABR), a wonderful organization, has many generous members who shared their knowledge with me, particularly Bob Davids, Jack Kavanagh, Pete Bjarkman, Tom Ruane, Ed Hartig, Lyle Spatz, Gerry Beirne, and Bill Deane. Others who lent great support and invaluable information include Mark Pollman, David Markson, Brian Mackerer, Jim Bouton, and the peerless one, Bert Sugar.

Races

If the game or situation is meaningless, players and teams have been known to let up on an opponent or help out a teammate. This happens as well with players vying for batting titles. In 1953 the American League batting race came down to the last day with Cleveland's Al Rosen and Washington's Mickey Vernon battling it out. The Senators were still playing when word came that Vernon would win the title by a point if he did not have to bat again. Conveniently, one Washington teammate was then picked off second following a double while another was thrown out trying to stretch a single.

Back in 1910 the AL batting race had also sparked some controversy. What happened and between whom?

The batting race was decided in the final days of the season when Detroit's Ty Cobb and Cleveland's Nap Lajoie were battling for the title. Cobb, easily the most hated player in the league, was in the lead. Cleveland was playing the St. Louis Browns on that final day and the St. Louis manager ordered rookie third baseman Red Corriden to play deep against Lajoie to give him a better chance to win the title. Lajoie collected eight hits in the doubleheader, six of them coming on "bunt" singles down the third base line and a triple that was "lost in the sun." It should have been enough to win the title for him but Cobb won the third of his nine straight titles with a .3850687 to .3840947 batting average. Cobb, however, was not always the fierce competitor, as he chose to sit out the last two games to preserve his average. St. Louis manager Jack O'Connor, who admitted helping Lajoie, was fired for his efforts.

Only recently was it discovered that a game in which Cobb went two-for-three was erroneously counted twice. The correction was made, and while Cobb is now listed with a lower 1910 average than Lajoie, he is still officially the batting champ.

In a similar situation, who did Chuck Klein beat out in a home run race?

Mel Ott. It was the next-to-last day of the 1929 season, and with the Cubs having clinched the pennant, the doubleheader between the Giants and Phils was meaningless. Meaningless except for the fact that the Giants' Mel Ott and the Phils' Chuck Klein were tied for the National League lead with 42 homers apiece. In the fifth inning of the opener, Klein followed a Lefty O'Doul home run with one of his own. It was to be his only hit of the game and his 43rd homer, breaking the tie and setting a new NL season record. Ott collected a walk and single in the first game, and singled in his first at bat in game two. Phils manager Burt Shotton, in a blatant display of shabby sportsmanship, then ordered Ott walked intentionally four straight times, and once semi-intentionally with the bases loaded. The following day against the Braves, Ott singled twice but lost the home run title 43–42.

How did Lou Gehrig "lose" the home run title in 1931?

From 1927 to 1930 Gehrig had finished a distant second to the Babe in the home run derby. But the gap was closing. Then on April 26, 1931, in a game in Washington, Gehrig came to bat with Lyn Lary on first and two out. Gehrig launched a drive to center that hit in the stands, bounced back out on the field, and was caught on the fly by the center fielder Harry Rice. The runner Lary looked up, saw Rice make the catch, and presumed Gehrig's hit was just a long fly for the inning's last out. So he headed for the dugout unnoticed by manager Joe McCarthy coaching at third, who was busy watching Gehrig circle the bases. Lou was then called out for passing the runner and he settled for a triple, forfeiting the home run. Gehrig ended the year tied with Ruth at 46 home runs each. Even though Lou also lost two RBIs in the game, he still led the Babe and the rest of the circuit with an awesome 184 runs knocked in.

The year 1954 featured a three-way batting race in the National League and a controversial call in the Junior Circuit batting race. Who was featured in each?

Going into the last day of the National League season, the Giants' Don Mueller was leading the batting race with a .3426 average, followed by Duke Snider at .3425 and Willie Mays at .3422. The Giants won in 11 innings against the Phils' Robin Roberts, and Mays collected three hits to win the title with a .345 average. Mueller slipped to .342 to edge Snider, who slipped to .341, for runner-up.

In the other league, Ted Williams broke his collarbone within minutes of taking the field in spring training and the 35-year-old slugger did not return to action until May 16. Then he did it with a bang, collecting eight hits in nine at bats and driving in seven runs in a doubleheader at Detroit. Williams hit .345 for the season, higher than the leader Bobby Avila at .341, but The Splinter was walked an AL-high 136 times and had only 386 official at bats. He was short of the then-needed total of 400 at bats. Because of the controversy, the rule was later changed to use plate appearances rather than times at bat. In all the seasons that Williams played when he was eligible for a batting title, only 12 hitters finished ahead of him.

Williams also missed a batting title on the last day of the 1949 season, the same day his Red Sox lost the pennant to the Yankees in a dramatic showdown at Yankee Stadium. In the 5–3 loss, Williams went hitless to finish the year at .3428. Meanwhile, Detroit's George Kell went two-for-three against the Browns to finish at .3429 and win the batting crown. The Browns used a different pitcher in each inning in the 4–3 loss to the Tigers.

What year featured the closest batting race in major league history?

The year was 1931 and the scene was the National League. Going into the last day of the season, the Cardinals had clinched the pennant in large part on the bats of Jim Bottomley and Chick Hafey, two of the league's top three hitters. Hafey, who had reported late because of a contract dispute, was hitting .353 before the start of the September 27 doubleheader

3

with the Reds. The Giants' Bill Terry, the top hitter in 1930, was four points behind. Hafey got only one hit in eight at bats in the twinbill, dropping his average to .3488. But Terry managed only a single in four at bats as the Giants lost 12–3 to Brooklyn, and he finished with a .3486 average. Jim Bottomley was a not-so-distant third with a .3482 average.

.400 Hitters

Every baseball fan knows that Ted Williams was the last batter to hit over .400 for a big league season. But who was the first? In each league?

In 1876, the National League's first season, Chicago second baseman Ross Barnes hit .429, far outdistancing everyone else including teammate Cap Anson, who hit .356. In 1901 Nap Lajoie, having jumped from the Phillies to Connie Mack's new AL entry, the Philadelphia Athletics, compiled the highest average for the league in this century. Lajoie's .422 (also listed in one record book as .426) topped all batters and served as one leg of the Triple Crown when the Frenchman also took RBI honors with 125 and a deadball-era home run title with 14.

When were both league batting titles won by champions hitting over .400 in the same season and in the same city and playing in the same home park?

We wouldn't have asked if George Sisler (.420) and Rogers Hornsby (.401) hadn't reached this height in 1922. Hornsby, in fact, in a five-year span between 1921 and 1925 *averaged* over .400, topping that mark three times and just missing twice. St. Louis fans were able to watch these two hitters at Sportsman's Park, the home field for both Sisler's Browns and Hornsby's Cardinals, since the Birds had vacated obsolete Robison Field in 1920.

Who has hit over .400 in this century and *not* won the batting title?

The best known example occurred in 1911 when Ty Cobb outhit Shoeless Joe Jackson to win his fifth batting title with a .420 average to rookie Jackson's .408. Despite a .356 lifetime average in a career cut short because of his alleged involvement in the fixing of the 1919 World Series, Jackson never won a batting title. Perhaps a born loser, he was surely a born runner-up, finishing second to Cobb in 1912 and 1913 as well.

The tables were turned on Cobb in 1922 when he hit .401 but still finished a distant second in the batting race to George Sisler's .420.

Only five times in major league history has a player hit over .400 in the same season he hit 20 home runs, and three times this feat was accomplished by Rogers Hornsby. Who did it the other two times?

Bill Terry and Ted Williams. Hornsby, the greatest right-handed hitter the game has seen, first set this mark in 1922 when he hit .401 with 42 home runs and 152 RBIs to win the Triple Crown. Two years later he hit .424 with 25 homers, and the following year won another Triple Crown with a .403 average, 39 homers, and 143 RBIs. Terry became the next player to achieve the feat when he hit 23 homers in 1930 to go with a .401 average. Williams hit .406 with 37 roundtrippers in 1941. Babe Ruth came close with a .393 and 41 homers in 1923, and more recently George Brett reached .390 with 24 homers in 1980.

Who was the last batter to hit .400 over 154 games?

Wade Boggs, and he did it through a 162-game stretch. Boggs has said many times that he thinks there will never be another .400 hitter like Williams, but the third baseman accomplished just that in 1985–86. Boggs hit .368 for the 1985 season, and followed with a .357 in 1986, but from June to June, the "hidden season" as sportswriter Chaz Scoggins called it, he hit .400.

After going hitless on June 12, 1985, Boggs was hitting just .300, but then he went on the hottest streak of his career and did not go hitless until July 26th. Over the final 107 games of 1985, he hit .402. In April 1986, he slumped a bit, but hit .471 for

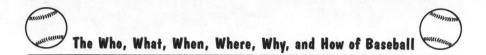

May to finish his streak of 154 games at .402. On June 8th, the 162nd game of his skein, he went hitless in three at bats against Tim Leary. So for the 162 games, Boggs played in 160 and hit an even .400, the only hitter since Williams to do it through a 154 (and 162) game stretch.

The peerless Tony Gwynn almost matched Boggs in a similar stretch played over the 1993 and 1994 seasons, but fell short, hitting .398 between the dates of July 1, 1993 and July 1, 1994.

Heavy Hitters

Joe Kelley had one of the most productive days in baseball history when on September 3, 1894, he went nine-for-nine in a doubleheader, including four doubles in one game. Kelley hit .393 that year and scored 165 runs for the champion Orioles. Who outscored him?

Billy Hamilton, another Hall of Famer. With pitchers still adjusting to the new distance of 60' 6", batters were teeing off in 1894, and none more than Philadelphia's wonderful quartet of outfielders. Tuck Turner hit .416 in 339 at bats, second best in the league, and he was a *backup* to the three other outfielders, Billy Hamilton (.399), Ed Delahanty (.400), and Sam Thompson (.404). All three are in the Hall of Fame. As a team, Philadelphia hit a record .349 that year, and Billy Hamilton scored an amazing 196 runs. Kelley's run total is the fifth highest in history—and he didn't even lead the league in 1894.

Who was the first player to collect 3,000 hits in his career?

Cap Anson, although the date he reached this mark is somewhat murky. The Hall of Famer was the premier manager of the nineteenth century but also was an outstanding performer with the White Stockings of the NL. This fiery, iron-willed athlete hit over .300 in all but three of his 22 seasons; won two batting titles, one with a .399 average; and led the NL in RBIs eight times. He holds the all-time record for errors for a first sacker, but this is due to his longevity and to playing in an era when players disdained mitts. As a manager he won nearly 1,300 games and in his first eight years at the helm guided Chicago to five pennants. A brilliant innovator, he devised the hit-and-run, was one of the first to call signals, developed the coaching box, and used relief pitchers and the pitching rotation. Often cited as a racist, he was still one of the prime reasons for baseball's early popularity. Anson was elected to the Hall of Fame in 1939.

Cap Anson reached the 3,000-hit mark without ever collecting 200 hits in a season. Only three other players have 3,000 career hits with no 200-hit seasons. Who are they?

Carl Yastrzemski, Dave Winfield, and Eddie Murray. Yaz played 23 years and though he twice led the league in hits, he never topped the 200 mark. His closest was 191 hits in 1962. Dave Winfield and Eddie Murray both had over 3,000 hits without collecting 200 in a season. Winfield missed by 7 hits in 1984, a year he hit a career-best .340.

Only three players have collected 200 hits in a season in each league. Who are these three post–WW II players?

The three players will probably be joined by others as free agency allows stars to switch teams and leagues. But for now, the only three are Bill Buckner, Steve Sax, and Al Oliver.

Buckner had 201 hits for the Cubs in 1982 and then went to the Red Sox in 1984 for Dennis Eckersley and Mike Brumley. The following year he again had 201 hits. Sax, the 1982 Rookie of the Year, had 210 hits for Los Angeles in 1986, then signed with the Yankees in 1988 as a free agent. The following year he nailed 205 hits. Oliver, the first player to ever accomplish the feat, collected 209 hits in 1980 with Texas, then went to Montreal in 1982 in a trade. That year he had 204 hits while collecting two legs of the Triple Crown.

Ty Cobb, the holder of the highest lifetime batting average at .367, is arguably the greatest hitter in baseball history. Upon retirement in 1928, the fierce competitor was the holder of 90 major league records and, in 1936, he was the highest vote-getter elected to the Hall of Fame. Between 1907 and 1919 he

dominated American League hitters, winning the batting title every year except one. What year did he lose the title and who beat him?

Tris Speaker was the hitter and 1916 was the year. Speaker hit .386 to Cobb's runner-up average of .371, the only season in 13 years that Cobb was not the loop's top hitter. As a player/manager in 1921, he was a runner-up to teammate Harry Heilmann, and in 1922 was a runner-up to George Sisler.

Eight times since 1900 the top hitter in one league has hit 50 points or higher than the top hitter in the other loop. Seven times it's been the American Leaguer who has led, and three times this feat was accomplished by Ty Cobb. Who were the three NL hitters that Cobb topped by 50 points or more?

In 1910, Cobb hit .385 to Sherry Magee's .331; the next year, he hit .420 to Honus Wagner's .334; and in 1919, his average was .384 to Edd Roush's .321. The lone National Leaguer to top the other circuit's hitter by more than 50 points was Cy Seymour in 1905. He hit .377 to Elmer Flick's .306.

The first year of the 1920s that Rogers Hornsby did *not* win the NL batting title was 1926. Who won the crown?

Bubbles Hargrave. The Cincinnati catcher led the way with a .353 and also led the NL in fielding with .988. Bubbles had only 326 at bats in 105 games, 93 behind the plate, but the rules at the time qualified him as batting champ. It wasn't until 1945 that the majors changed the rule to 400 at bats. One reference book, however, lists rookie Paul Waner as the 1926 winner at .336. Bubbles, whose brother Pinky also played in the majors, ended his 12-year career with a .310 average.

Bubbles Hargrave was the first catcher to win a batting title, and only one other catcher has led the league in hitting since. Who was the player?

Hall of Famer Ernie Lombardi twice won batting titles despite his legendary lack of speed. The big catcher played in over 100 games for ten straight years with the Reds, hitting over .300 in seven of them. Twice he led the NL in fielding, and he won the Most Valuable Player Award in 1938 when he led the league in hitting with a .342 average. Following a trade to the Braves in 1942, he won his second batting title with a .330 average.

One of the first Italian-Americans to star in the major leagues, this San Francisco native once hit 60 home runs in a minor league season. In the majors he would win five World Championships as a member of the New York Yankees, drive in 100 or more runs seven times, and set an AL record with 11 RBIs in one game. Who was the player?

Tony Lazzeri. In 1925 Lazzeri hit 60 home runs, drove in an incredible 222 runs, and scored a still-standing pro record 202 runs for Salt Lake City in the Pacific Coast League. A stellar accomplishment, even if done in a 197-game schedule. Nicknamed "Poosh 'em up," Lazzeri was a prominent member of the Murderers' Row and was the Yankees' starting second baseman from 1926 to 1937. He was elected to the Hall of Fame in 1991.

En route to his 11-RBI game on May 24, 1936, Lazzeri became the first player ever to hit two grand slams in one game, a feat that has been equaled eight times since. Who is the *only* National Leaguer to hit two grand slams in one game?

Tony Cloninger. Cloninger was a pitcher for the Atlanta Braves, and on July 3, 1966, he belted two grand slams against the San Francisco Giants. He finished the day with nine RBIs, the all-time record for pitchers.

Jim Bottomley, playing for the Cardinals, set the single-game record with 12 RBIs in 1924. Bottomley's mark, in a 17–3 win against Brooklyn on September 16, 1924, came on three singles, a double and two home runs. This record was finally equaled in 1993, and by another Cardinal. Who did it?

Mark Whiten, a third-year outfielder for St. Louis, tied Bottomley's record on September 7, 1993, in the second game of a doubleheader against the Reds, a 15–2 rout. His four homers also tied the record. In the first game, which the Reds won 14–13 as Whiten misplayed a ball into a two-run triple, he had another RBI—giving him 13 for the day.

Five years later, Whiten's Cleveland team found itself on the short end of an 11–2 contest against the Oakland A's. With his bullpen strapped from a 17-inning loss the night before, Indians manager Mike Hargrove called on Whiten to hold the fort. The former college hurler faced seven batters in his inning of work, allowing one run on a double, walk, hit batsman and walk. The three batters he retired all went down on strikes, making Whiten the only pitcher in major league history, with at least one inning pitched, who recorded all of his outs on strikeouts.

Another slugger, Rocky Colavito, who once hit four homers in a game, made two appearances as a pitcher, 10 years apart. In 1958, the cannon-armed outfielder hurled three hitless innings of relief for the Cleveland Indians in a game against Detroit. Ten years later, on August 25, 1968, Colavito tossed 2.2 scoreless innings for the Yankees, also against the Tigers. "The Rock" homered that day and picked up the win in relief. Since position players are usually only used in games in which their team is hopelessly behind, Colavito's victory is especially noteworthy. Counting Rocky's two stints with the Indians, he and Whiten are the only two players to club four homers in a game and play for six teams.

Several noteworthy pitching performances have been turned in by other position players forced into action on the mound. First baseman-outfielder Larry Biittner didn't quite match Whiten's feat, but he did strike out three of the batters he faced in 1.1 innings of work in relief in his only appearance on the mound, for the 1977 Chicago Cubs. Unfortunately, he gave up home runs to three others. Biittner was later fined $50 by the NL for throwing a "brush-back" pitch after surrendering the three home runs, but his teammates took up a collection to pay for his shave.

What player collected all six of his career RBIs in one game?

Detroit pitcher Babe Birrer lived up to his nickname when, on July 19, 1955, he came on in relief against the Baltimore Orioles and threw four shutout innings to pick up the win. He also clouted two three-run homers in his only two at bats. He might as well have burned his bat then, because the Babe played in 55 other games between 1955 and 1958 and never had another ribbie.

Orel Hershiser, one of the best-hitting pitchers in recent years, spent 1993 pursuing the single-season hitting record for National League pitchers. He finished with a .356 to fall short of the old mark. Whose record was he after?

Jack Bentley's. One of the most intriguing players ever, the 18-year-old Bentley pitched three games for Washington in 1913 and soon after went to the minors. He starred for the minor league Baltimore Orioles and owner Jack Dunn, the man who sold Babe Ruth to the Red Sox. In 1921 he led the International League with a .412 average, hit 24 homers, and had a 12–1 record as a pitcher. The following year he played in every game either on the mound or at first base, hit .351 and had a 1.73 ERA with a 13–2 record. He finally made it back to the majors with the Giants when John McGraw agreed to pay a record $72,000 to Dunn for the star. McGraw refused to put Bentley in the outfield, but as a pinch hitter/pitcher he compiled a 13–8 mark, while hitting his NL-record .427. Ten of his 38 hits came as a pinch hitter. He was finished after the 1927 season, retiring with a 46–33 pitching record and a .291 career batting average.

The peerless Walter Johnson had a lifetime batting average of .236 and was often called upon to pinch hit. In 1925, at the age of 38, The Big Train hit .433 in 97 at bats, a highwater mark for pitchers in the Junior Circuit. He also was 20–7 for the pennant-winning Senators.

What is more rare than a no-hitter? Hitting for the cycle. Collecting a single, double, triple, and home run in the same game occurs less frequently than a no-hitter. When Travis Fryman hit for the cycle in 1993 (he added another double for good measure), he was the first Tiger since Hoot Evers in 1950 to accomplish it. A handful of players have done it twice in their careers, but only one player in each league has hit for the cycle three times. Who are they?

In the American League, it's Bob Meusel who cycled three times in the 1920s while playing for the Yankees. The other name on the list is the Babe—Herman that is. Herman did it twice as a Dodger in 1931, the third time with the Cubs in 1933. Babe Ruth? He never did hit for the cycle.

In the 20th century only 14 regulars have had seasons in which they collected more walks than hits. Max Bishop did it five seasons in the American League, and in the NL Eddie Stanky drew more free passes than hits twice. Gene Tenace did it in each league and came the closest to anyone in doing it for a career, 1,060 hits and 984 walks. Often these patient batters looking for a walk are less likely to be .300 hitters. Who are the only two players to hit over .300 in a season while collecting more walks than hits?

Ted Williams and Mickey Mantle each did it once.

In 1954 Williams broke his collarbone in spring training and ended up playing in just 117 games. The Splinter hit a league-high .345 and collected 136 walks to go with his 133 hits. But he lost the batting title to Bobby Avila, who hit .341, because of the 1945 rule which stated that a player needed 400 at bats to win the title. Williams missed by 14 at bats. In 1962 Mantle had just 377 at bats but collected a league-high 122 walks, one more than his number of hits. His average was .321.

Babe Ruth has the most walks in a career with 2,056, but not until his last, short stay with the Boston Braves did he have more walks than hits. He was hitting .181 when he quit on June 2, 1935.

The patient and powerful Mark McGwire, in 1998, had 152 hits while being walked an NL-record 162 times. Mac was three-for-three, including his 70th homer, on his final day to almost hit .300, finishing the year at .299.

A forgotten player, Dave Rowan, hit .385 in 18 games for the 1911 St. Louis Browns, collecting 11 RBIs in just 65 at bats. But Rowan wasn't invited back the following season, thus allowing him to set the record for highest career batting average (minimum 50 at bats). That was a record until this player came along. Labeled "a fat tub of goo" by David Letterman, who is he?

Terry Forster. A phenom at 18, he pitched just 10 games in A-ball in 1970 and made the White Sox the following April. In 1972 he set a club record with 29 saves and was the AL Fireman of the Year in 1974. A sore arm slowed his fastball, and he was traded to Pittsburgh. He later went west as a free agent, the Dodgers' first. He had 22 saves and a 1.94 ERA for the pennant winners in 1978. While Forster could pitch and eat, he was certainly a stellar hitter. In the last year before the designated hitter rule, he batted .526, and finished with a career average of .397, the highest ever.

On the other end of the spectrum are hitters like Dean Chance, who owns the worst batting average (minimum 500 at bats) ever with an .066, and Bob Buhl, who went to the plate 70 times in 1962 with nary a hit. What player, from the 1960s and '70s, has the worst career average *ever* for a player with at least 100 at bats?

Ron Herbel. The chunky part-time starter for the Giants, Herbel batted just .029 (6-for-206). He led the NL in relief appearances in 1970 with 75 while pitching for the Padres and Mets.

Who is the worst hitter with a minimum of 2,500 at bats?

Bill Bergen, who caught for the Reds and the Dodgers between 1901 and 1911, is the worst hitter ever to play regularly. By far. His .170 career average is 42 points below the next worst hitter. He had only one season over .200 and in 1909 had a .132 average, the lowest mark ever for a player qualifying for the batting title. That same year, however, he had 202 assists and on August 23 he threw out six would-be base stealers, a modern record.

If most of the strikeout pitchers are recent, it stands that the hitters who strike out the most are contemporaries. And so it is. Rob Deer, who bowed out after the 1993 season leads by averaging one strikeout for less than three times at bat; the next 40 flailers on the futility list all average a strikeout for every three-to-five times at bat. All the top 40 swingers with a minimum of 1,000 games played in the 1960s or later—all but one. Which batter was ahead of his time?

Vince DiMaggio. The oldest of the three brothers, Vince played in the majors for 10 years, eight of them as a starter. He led the NL in strikeouts in six of those years, including 134 K's in 1938, a major league record he's since given up. A good fielder and baserunner, Vince played in two All-Star Games and collected a homer, triple and single in the 1943 Classic.

Batting Titles

Who is the only batting champion to win a title in three different decades?

Logic tells you the answer oughta be Cobb, but it's not. Cobb won his first title in 1907 and, except for the year 1916, won every single American League batting title through the 1919 season. The Georgia Peach hit .357 over the next nine seasons, including .401 in 1922, but not once did he lead the league. Besides Joe Jackson, Cobb is the only one to hit .400 without winning the batting title.

The only player to accomplish the feat of winning batting titles in three decades is George Brett, who won in 1976 (.333), 1980 (.390), and 1990 (.329). Like Cobb, Brett won his first title by beating out a teammate, and not without controversy. His bloop hit in the season finale bounced in front of Twins outfielder Steve Brye and skipped over his head for an inside-the-park homer. The hit gave Brett the title by a point over teammate Hal McRae, who initially thought the misplay was deliberate and charged the Twins with racism. He later changed his mind.

Brett's last title came in the same year that Nolan Ryan threw his sixth no-hitter to become the first pitcher to throw no-hitters in three different decades. This would have been too easy a question on its own, but we couldn't let it slip by unnoticed. No three-decade answer would be complete without including shortstop Luis Aparicio, the only player to win a Gold Glove in three decades.

One player won his second batting title in the 1950s, one of four decades in which he wore a major league uniform as a player. A seven-time All-Star, he led the league in doubles three times and fielding percentage four times. Who was it?

Mickey Vernon won his first batting title in 1946 and his second, at the age of 35, in 1953, beating out Al Rosen on the last day of the season. When he retired in 1960 the popular Vernon managed the Washington Senators from 1961 through 40 games in 1963.

Mickey Vernon was one of seven players who won two batting titles and yet had a career batting average under .300. Who are the other six, all of whom won their silver bats after WW II?

Ferris Fain won consecutive AL batting titles in 1951 (.344) and 1952 (.327), the only two full seasons he hit over .300. The good-fielding first sacker had a career average of .290, though his real value was getting on base—his career on base percentage was .425.

Tommy Davis also won consecutive titles in 1962–63 for the Dodgers. In 1962 he added 153 RBIs, the most in the NL in 25 years, to his 230 hits. He had six .300+ seasons but injuries cut his lifetime average down to .294.

Pete Runnels led the AL in hitting in 1960 (.320) and 1962 (.326), after having almost won the title in 1958. With two days left, Runnels and his teammate Ted Williams had exactly the same batting average, but Pete went three-for-ten while Williams was five-for-eight. Williams ended with a .328 average while Runnels closed out at .322. For his lifetime, Runnels was a .291 hitter. Carl Yastrzemski led the league three times (1963, 1967, 1968) in hitting and added the Triple Crown in 1967. In 1968, "The Year of the Pitcher," his .301 average was the lowest ever to win a title. Yaz hit .285 for his 23 years.

Dave Parker won consecutive NL titles in 1977 (.338) and 1978 (.334) and wound up with a .290 career average. The last name on the list is Willie McGee, who won two batting titles (1985, 1990) and has a career average under .300.

Several good guesses might have included Al Kaline and Mickey Mantle. Mantle led in 1956 and was second to Williams in 1957, despite hitting .365. The 20-year-old Kaline hit .340 in

1955, then finished second in batting in 1959, 1961, and 1963. Both Hall of Famers hit below .300 for their careers.

And you may wonder just who is the player with the highest career average *without* a .300 season (ten seasons of at least 100 at bats)? Answer: Sam Mertes (.279), who toiled at the turn of the twentieth century. Of strictly 20th century players, the list is headed by Mookie Wilson and Jim Gantner, both of whom hit .274.

Besides Mickey Vernon, seven other players who performed in the 1950s played in three other decades as well. Who were they?

For a correct answer in the four-decade category the requirement usually is that a player starts as one decade closes, plays another 20 years, and ends his career within a year or two in the fourth decade. And so it is here:

Jim Kaat (1959–1983)
Tim McCarver (1959–1980)
Willie McCovey (1959–1980)
Minnie Minoso (1949–1980)
Bobo Newsom (1929–1953)
Ted Williams (1939–1960)
Early Wynn (1939–1963)

Though he retired in 1964, Minoso actually played in five decades, having been brought out of retirement by Bill Veeck 12 years later as a DH against Frank Tanana on September 11, 1976. He went hitless that game but the next day collected his last major league hit. In 1980 he made two more appearances at bat to join Nick Altrock as the only five-decade player, but then was barred from any more major league at bats by the commissioner. In 1993, however, he appeared in a minor league game.

Elmer Valo, who, according to the record books, made his first appearance in the big leagues in 1940, actually appeared in the A's last game of 1939. Valo got a walk, but then his name was removed from the official box score at the behest of Connie Mack. Mack had failed to sign Valo to a major league contract and the official scorer obliged. Valo refuses to confirm or deny the story but Red Smith told this author the anecdote—and Smith was the official scorer that day! Valo retired in 1961.

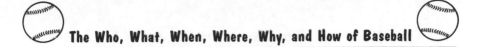

Continuing the four-decade-player questions, what players performed in the 1960s, 1970s, 1980s, and 1990s?

Only four. Nolan Ryan, who came up in 1966 and retired in 1993, is one obvious answer. The others include Bill Buckner, who broke in with the Dodgers in 1969 as an outfielder and ended his career 22 years later with the Red Sox in 1990. Carlton Fisk came up with Boston in 1969 and retired, albeit reluctantly, in 1993. Jerry Reuss is the last. Reuss pitched one game in 1969, four in 1990, and 623 in between, winning 220 regular-season games. Jerry was less successful in post-season play, going 0–7 in league championship play, the only pitcher to drop that many.

A few others came close to four decades. Darrell Evans started in 1969 and still played in more than 100 games in 1989, but chose to retire rather than go into his fourth decade. Another Evans, Dwight, played into the 1990s, but did not come up to the Red Sox until 1972.

Who is the only utility player ever to win a batting title?

Billy Goodman was the Red Sox's starting first baseman when the 1950 season opened, but after chipping an ankle he missed three weeks. When he returned, Walt Dropo had taken over first on his way to Rookie of the Year honors. Goodman filled in at short for a game, then took over third base for two weeks when Johnny Pesky was injured. His big chance came as a result of Ted Williams' injury while making a leaping catch in the All-Star Game. Williams shattered his elbow and was sidelined till September. Goodman took over left field with the Red Sox in fourth place. Boston went 44–17 in the Splinter's absence and Goodman hit .370 in the stretch. When Williams returned to regular action in mid-September, Sox fans were hopeful, but a pennant was not to be. Meanwhile, Pesky offered to sit down to allow Goodman a regular spot in the lineup, and the lanky line drive hitter ended the year at .354, the only utility player to win a batting title.

Who hit safely in the most games during a season and how many games was it?

The answer, as researched by Allen Lewis, is 135 games, a mark shared by three players: Wade Boggs (1985), Chuck Klein

(1930) and Rogers Hornsby (1922). Hornsby was hitless in just 19 games that year, while Klein went hitless in 21 and Boggs in 26. Rod Carew, who hit .388 in 1977, is next on the list, hitting in 131 games out of 155 played, followed by George Sisler in 1920, who hit in 130 out of the 154 he played. Williams in his 1941 season got into 143 games and, despite being walked 145 times, went hitless in just 22 games.

Joe DiMaggio's record 56-game hitting streak was chased by Pete Rose in 1978, the first serious threat to the streak in decades. What was Rose's eventual season total and whose National League record did he break?

Forty-four games. Pistol Pete collected his 3,000th hit on May 5 against Steve Rogers, but by June 13, when he was held hitless, his average stood at .267. He didn't go hitless again until August. On July 25 he collected three hits to break Tommy Holmes's modern NL record of 37 straight games, and on July 31 he singled off Phil Niekro to tie Willie Keeler's 81-year-old NL record of 44 games. The following day Rose went hitless against the Braves, and ended the year with a .302 average.

Wee Willie Keeler was a key member of the old Oriole and Brooklyn dynasty, hitting .378 over an eight-year period. In 1897 he hit .424, the fourth highest mark in major league history, and collected hits in 44 straight games. Keeler did have one advantage over Rose in that foul balls were not considered strikes until four years later.

Another 19th century star, Bill Dahlen set the record that Keeler broke by hitting in 42 straight games in 1894, the year the pitchers were moved back to their present distance. After being held hitless on August 7, Dahlen reeled off another 28-game streak, thus hitting in 70 of 71 games.

Switch-Hitters

Babe Ruth holds the record for home runs by a left-handed hitter, while Hank Aaron holds the record for righties. Who is the top slugger among switch-hitters?

Mickey Mantle. The Mick crashed 536 home runs, tops for switch-hitters, his last one coming on September 20, 1968, batting left-handed against the Red Sox's Jim Lonborg. Mantle hit 373 homers left-handed, 163 right-handed. Reflecting a trend, Mantle is the only player among the ten switch-hitting home run leaders to play before 1966.

Who holds the record for most games with homers from each side of the plate?

Mickey Mantle did it in ten games, a record that stood until 1994 when Eddie Murray hit switch-homers in a game for the 11th time. Not surprisingly, it is Murray who is the runner-up to Mantle on the all time list of switch-hitting sluggers, though the future Hall of Famer has already passed Mantle in RBIs. In April 1993 switch-hitter Carlos Baerga did something that the Mick and Murray never did, nor anyone else; he hit two homers in one inning, one from each side of the plate.

In 1973 Pete Rose's 230 hits set a major league record for switch-hitters. Which player tied that record in 1980?

Kansas City Royals' outfielder Willie Wilson rapped 230 hits in 1980, tying Rose's record for switch-hitters. Wilson collected 130 hits left-handed and 100 hits right-handed, making him the only American Leaguer ever to get at least 100 hits from each side of the plate in one season.

Pete Rose is one of 18 players with 3,000 career hits, though only 160 of those were home runs. Which two players have 3,000 hits and more than 500 home runs?

Willie Mays (660) and Hank Aaron (755). Actually, they both have more than 600 home runs, but that would have made the question too easy.

The career leader in hits with 4,256, Pete Rose had a record ten seasons in which he collected 200 hits or more. Pete had 230 hits in his MVP year in 1973 when he led the league in hitting with a .338 average. Since Rose, two NL switch-hitters have won MVP honors, the Cardinals' Willie McGee in 1985, and the Braves' Terry Pendleton in 1991. Who was the last switch-hitting American Leaguer to win that honor?

A knuckleball. The last AL switch-hitter to win the MVP was pitcher Vida Blue, who copped the honors in 1971 when he won 24 games and led the league in ERA with a nifty 1.82. Blue was named the Cy Young winner as well, as he led Oakland to the Western Division championship. Blue, who was a switch-hitter, hit a lusty .118 that year, slightly above his career average, and better than his rookie year when he hit zero as a lefty. The only other switch-hitter to win an AL MVP? Mickey Mantle.

One Hall of Fame hitter began his minor league career as a pitcher before switching positions. In 1952 he made his one major league appearance as a pitcher. Who was it and what was the occasion?

The hurler was Stan Musial, who had begun his career as a minor league pitcher before what must have been a heaven-sent injury forced him to the outfield. For much of 1952 it was a two-man batting race in the Senior Circuit between Musial and the Cubs' Frankie Baumholtz. By late September, however, Musial had pulled away and had his sixth batting title sewn up. So on September 29, the last game of the season, the Cardinals were facing the Cubs, and, with a pre-game handshake agreement, the left-handed Musial took the mound to face the leadoff hitter

Baumholtz. Baumholtz, usually a lefty, batted right-handed for the first time in his life, and smashed a grounder off third sacker Solly Hemus's knee for an error. "Probably the hardest liner I ever hit," Baumholtz commented later. Rookie Harvey Haddix then relieved Musial.

Designated Hitters

Who was John Heydler and why is he associated with the designated hitter rule?

John Heydler was the president of the National League from 1918 to 1934 and was instrumental in helping establish baseball's Hall of Fame. At the 1928 National League meeting in December, Heydler proposed that a designated hitter rule be instituted to speed up the game. He said that fans were tired of seeing weak-hitting pitchers come to the plate, and the DH would inject some needed scoring into the offense. Heydler's proposal was backed by the influential John McGraw but when it was brought up the following week in a joint meeting of the two leagues, the American League flatly rejected the idea of the designated hitter.

The notion of the designated hitter was around even earlier than the 1920s, almost as early as the start of the American League. When Connie Mack proposed it in 1906, the Philadelphia *North American* said, "the suggestion, often made . . . has been brought up again."

On Opening Day, 1973, a Yankee made history when he became the first designated hitter ever to bat in a regular-season game. He also became the first designated hitter to drive in a run, drawing a bases-loaded walk off Red Sox pitcher Luis Tiant in the top half of the first inning. He would eventu-

ally retire with a .293 career batting average. Who was the pinstriper?

Ron Blomberg. Blomberg hit a career-high .329 with 12 home runs in 1973 while splitting his playing time between DH and first base. Hampered by injuries throughout his career, he played just 461 games in his eight major league seasons, 177 as a DH.

Designated hitters are usually known more for their power than their speed. Who is the first DH ever to steal 20 bases in one season?

Paul Molitor. Molitor stole 23 bases as the Milwaukee Brewers' designated hitter in 1987, then broke his own record with 24 in 1992. In 1994, Molitor swiped 20 bases without being caught, an American League record. And on August 8, 1998, the 42-year-old Molitor flashed his vintage form by going 5-for-5 and swiping his 500th base. His season record was broken in 1998 by Jose Canseco, who had 29 as the DH with Toronto.

Since the designated hitter rule was instituted, only one pitcher has started a game as the DH. Who was it?

On June 11, 1988, pitcher Rick Rhoden started for the Yankees as the DH, and hit a sacrifice fly in an 8–6 win over Baltimore. A year later, he ended his 16-year career with a .238 average.

Doubles and Triples

No one has ever led the league in doubles, triples, *and* home runs. Several players came close, including George Sisler in 1920 and Lou Gehrig in 1927, both of whom led in doubles and were second in homers and triples. Ty Cobb missed by just three home runs in 1908 and 1911 and two homers in 1917. Who came the closest to achieving this feat?

Stan Musial in 1948. Stan the Man did everything but sell popcorn for the Cards that year. He had 39 home runs, just one behind coleaders Ralph Kiner and Johnny Mize, but he led in nearly every other offensive category including slugging, batting, hits, doubles, triples, RBIs, and total bases.

Ted Williams didn't do it, and neither did Mickey Mantle. Collect 400 total bases in a single season, that is. Babe Ruth was the first to top the mark, in 1921, after the introduction of the livelier ball, and both he and Lou Gehrig teamed up in 1927 to top the 400 base plateau. Gehrig did it five times, but only five American Leaguers and nine National Leaguers have done it. In 1937, Joe DiMaggio reached that height, while in the NL Joe Medwick accomplished it as he collected the Triple Crown. But since 1937 only five players have collected 400 total bases in a season. Name the sluggers.

Stan Musial, Jim Rice, Hank Aaron, Larry Walker, and Sammy Sosa.

The 400 total base mark is one of the toughest for a hitter, and only 14 in history have topped the mark. Stan Musial cracked 429 total bases in his MVP year of 1948, while Hank

26

Aaron just reached the 400-base mark in 1959, thanks to playing two losing games in the NL playoffs with Los Angeles. Jim Rice led the AL in a number of categories in 1978, including hits (213), homers (46), triples (15), RBIs (139), and slugging (.600). In 1997 Larry Walker topped the NL charts in homers (49) and slugging (.720), while leading in total bases. In Sosa's incredible 66-homer season of 1998, a season in which he totaled 416 bases, he led the Senior Circuit in runs scored (132) and RBIs (158). In fact, Sosa, along with McGwire in 1998, joined Babe Ruth as the only batters to knock in a hundred runs in a season just on homers. Ruth did it twice.

Albert Belle just missed the magic mark in 1998, falling one shy with 399 total bases. Three years earlier, Belle was in a league of his own, collecting 377 total bases in the strike-shortened season.

Others reaching 400 total bases are:

AL Players	Year	Total Bases	NL Players	Year	Total Bases
Babe Ruth	1921	457	Rogers Hornsby	1922	450
Lou Gehrig	1927	447	Chuck Klein	1930	445
Jimmie Foxx	1932	438	Stan Musial	1948	429
Lou Gehrig	1930	419	Hack Wilson	1930	423
Joe DiMaggio	1937	418	Sammy Sosa	1998	416
Babe Ruth	1927	417	Larry Walker	1997	409
Lou Gehrig	1931	410	Chuck Klein	1929	405
Lou Gehrig	1934	409	Hank Aaron	1959	400
Jim Rice	1978	406			
Hal Trosky	1936	405			
Jimmie Foxx	1933	403			
Lou Gehrig	1936	403			

Which hitter holds the single-season record for doubles?

Boston Red Sox left fielder Earl Webb set the record in 1931 when he slammed out a total of 67. His previous high was achieved the year before when he cracked 30. The lanky left-hander's total can't all be blamed on the Fenway's Green Monster, since the high left field wall wasn't constructed till 1934. There was, however, a tall facade in left that helped Webb, and he was also accused of occasionally pulling up at second base on sure triples. Still, Earl Webb is the top man for doubles in a single season.

How about the single season record for triples?

A tough one. It's the Pirates' Owen Wilson in 1912 with 36, the most ever in professional baseball, and an amazing ten ahead of the next 20th century major league player. Playing in gigantic Forbes Field, the lefty Wilson hit 24 of his 36 triples there, and his teammates chipped in with another 93 to set a modern major league team record. In the 20th century, the Pirates have led the league in triples 40 times, while finishing second in triples 23 times. But since abandoning Forbes Field in 1970, only two Pirates, Omar Moreno (1980) and Andy Van Slyke (1988), have led the league in triples.

In 1947 Jake Jones collected a triple on a foul ball. How did he do it?

Jones, a journeyman first baseman playing for the Red Sox, hit a dribbler down the third base line against the Browns. Pitcher Fred Sanford, running over to pick up the ball, saw that it had rolled foul, and threw his mitt at it. Citing the rule about intentionally thrown gloves, umpire Cal Hubbard awarded Jones a triple. The rule was changed in 1954 to apply only to balls in fair territory.

When were ground rule doubles considered home runs?

Until 1930 a fair ball that bounced into the stands was counted as a home run. That year the American League changed the rule to make the hit a ground-rule double, and the National League followed a year later. Baseball historian Bob Davids estimates that some 10 to 20 "bounce homers" occurred each season, with park architecture being the obvious deciding factor.

Tiger pitcher Eddie Summers, a .162 lifetime swatter, hit only two homers in his career, both in a September 17, 1910 game, and both were bounce homers. In 1927 the Waner brothers each hit a bounce homer at Cincinnati's Redland Field, and each came in the same inning! That same year Gehrig hit one of his two career bounce home runs, but Ruth bounced none of his 714 into the stands. According to Davids, the last official "bounce" home run probably came on September 10, 1930, when the Dodgers' Al Lopez clubbed a ball over Bob Meusel's head and it bounced into the Ebbets Field stands.

Harry Lumley led the PCL in batting in 1903 and was signed by Brooklyn for the 1904 season. The rookie continued his good hitting by leading the loop in home runs (9) and triples (18). Since then, only four players have led the league in both categories and two did it the same year. Can you name the quartet?

The four are Jim Bottomley in 1928, Mickey Mantle and Willie Mays in 1955, and Jim Rice in 1978. All but Rice are in the Hall of Fame.

There have been a number of players who made one appearance in the majors and then were gone. Teenager John Paciorek, whose brothers Jim and Tom were big leaguers— Tom for 18 years—went three-for-three with two walks in his one-game major league career. He returned to the minors in 1964 and his career ended a few years after he underwent a spinal fusion to correct a back problem. He is the only player with three hits and a 1.000 batting average. Who is the only player to hit two triples in his one big league game?

The answer is Ed Irvin, briefly a Detroit Tiger, who hit his two triples on May 18, 1912. But the circumstances surrounding his lone appearance are more interesting than the feat.

On May 15 the Tigers were in New York for a game when an iron-lunged fan named Claude Lucker harassed Detroit's Ty Cobb. Cobb put up with it for a few innings and then went into the stands and beat him up even after he discovered Lueker was crippled. Other fans quickly joined in and the Tiger players charged the stands to defend their star player. Order was eventually restored but Ban Johnson, the American League president, suspended Cobb indefinitely. Cobb, who the previous year had led the AL in every offensive category except home runs, was not popular with his teammates, but without him they had no chance for a pennant. A telegram of protest to the imperious Johnson went unheeded, so the players voted to strike. Johnson reacted by proclaiming he would slap a fine of $5,000 on the

Tigers unless they fielded a team, so Tigers owner Frank Navin quickly ordered manager Hugh Jennings to field a team or else. The Tigers were in Philadelphia to play the Athletics, and Jennings went looking around the city for nine warm bodies.

Starting the game for Detroit that May 18 was a motley crew headed by Detroit coaches Joe Sugden, 41, and Jim McGuire, 48. The other seven included a few college players and local amateurs, including Ed Irvin. Irvin had two triples in three at bats to close out his career with a slugging average of 2.000. Starter Aloysius Travers pitched a complete game against the A's but gave up 24 runs on 26 hits in eight innings to seal his fate. Only one player, Billy Maharg (whose real name was Graham, "Maharg" reversed), ever appeared again in the majors. Maharg, a hanger-on and gofer for some of the Philadelphia players, got into one game in 1916 for the Phillies, and then resurfaced in 1919 as a conspirator in the Black Sox scandal.

Ban Johnson met with the Tigers the following day and told them that they had better play in Washington on the 20th or they would never play again. Led by Cobb, the team went back to work. Cobb was fined just $50 for the incident, and suspended for another week, while Johnson slapped a $100 fine on each of the Tiger players who signed the telegram of protest.

In 1912, Hall of Famer Tris Speaker hit 53 doubles and had 52 stolen bases for the Boston Red Sox. Who is the only other player this century to reach 50 steals and 50 doubles in the same year?

Houston's great Craig Biggio accomplished this in 1998. Biggio hit 51 doubles and on September 23 against the Cardinals he stole his 50th base to join Tris Speaker.

One other 50-50 mark stood until 1995. In that strike-shortened year, Albert Belle reached the 50-50 mark in homers and doubles, accomplishing it in just 144 games. He is the first to reach that level.

Home Runs

The 1961 Yankees were one of the greatest slugging teams in baseball history. Paced by Roger Maris's record 61 homers and Mickey Mantle's 54, the Bronx Bombers pounded out a major league record 240 roundtrippers. Six players on the '61 Yankees hit 20 or more home runs, a league record that was matched just three years later by the Twins, a team that finished tied for sixth place, and again by the 1986 Tigers. Which players formed the slugging sextet on the 1961 Yankees?

The six were Roger Maris (61), Mickey Mantle (54), Moose Skowron (28), Yogi Berra (22), Elston Howard (21), and John Blanchard (21). Blanchard and Skowron are the only two of the six whose numbers have not been retired by the Yankees.

The 1953 Giants were the first National League squad to have five players with 20 or more homers, a mark that was equaled by the Reds and the Cubs within five years. But only one NL team has ever had six players hit out 20 or more homers in a single season. Which is the team and the sextet with 20 homers?

The 1965 Braves, in their last season in Milwaukee, had six sluggers with 20 or more dingers. Eddie Mathews and Hank Aaron, each with 32, Mack Jones (31), Joe Torre (27), Felipe Alou (23), and Gene Oliver (21). Aaron would have hit 33, but a homer on August 18 was nullified when the ump ruled that Aaron's foot was out of the box when he made contact.

The 1947 New York Giants banged out a then NL record 221 homers, but had just four players with over 20 homers.

When young Shane Spencer hit ten homers in just 67 at-bats for the record-setting Yankees, he became the tenth Yankee to reach double figures in 1998. The ten with ten or more is a new record.

Who is the only Hall of Famer to hit more than 400 homers but never have a 40-homer season?

Stan Musial. The popular Musial hit 475 home runs over a 22-year career to rank 16th on the all-time list, and yet he never led the league in homers. His high was 39 home runs in 1948, when he finished behind Ralph Kiner and Johnny Mize, who each had 40. That year Musial led in practically everything else, including selling tickets, topping the NL in hits, doubles, triples, batting and slugging averages, and RBIs to win his third MVP. His 474th home run in 1963 came on the day he became a grandfather.

Dave Winfield and Eddie Murray are also over the 400-homer mark without hitting 40 in a season. After hitting 20 homers as a Padre in 1974, Winfield had 15 seasons of 20+ homers. His highest total was 37 in 1982 with the New York Yankees. Murray had 17 seasons with 20+ homers; his high-water mark came in 1983 when he hit 33. The durable Murray racked up 20 consecutive seasons in which he knocked in at least 75 runs. In 1996, he surpassed Hank Aaron, who had a string of 19 seasons with 75+ ribbies.

Jose Canseco took the mound in 1993 in an ill-fated relief appearance against the Red Sox (a 15–1 loss by the Rangers). Pitching just days after a ball had bounced off his head and over the fence for a 7–6 loss, Canseco strained his shoulder, putting him out of action. It was not, of course, the first time a slugger with 40 homers toed a pitching rubber. Babe Ruth was a marvelous pitcher who finished his mound career with a 6–5 complete game win against the Red Sox at the end of the 1933 season, knocking a homer to help his own cause. What other sluggers with 40-homer seasons have pitched in the majors?

Other celebrated swatters who got to pitch include Jimmie Foxx, Rocky Colavito, and Dave Kingman. Jimmie Foxx, old

Double X, pitched in ten games and compiled a nifty 1.52 ERA in 24 innings. He won his only decision at the age of 37 in 1945. Rocky Colavito gave up no runs in two appearances, while Big Dave Kingman pitched four innings in mop-up action for the 1973 Giants. He walked six, gave up three hits, but K'd four batters.

After switching to first base, George Sisler took the mound several times, including two occasions when the opposing pitcher was Ty Cobb! The last time was an end-of-the-season stunt in 1925, when, on October 4th, Cobb pitched a scoreless inning while Sisler went two scoreless frames. The two future Hall of Famers were managers at the time.

When this slugger retired he had 442 home runs and twice led the league in roundtrippers. He is the first hitter with more than 400 homers *not* to be elected to the Hall of Fame when he became eligible. Who was it?

One thing Dave Kingman could do was hit homers. He couldn't hit for an average (lifetime .236) or play defense, or get along with fans or sportswriters, but he could crank them out of the park. His best season came in 1979 with the Cubs when he hit .288 with 48 homers. In 1977 Big Dave set a modern record by playing for four teams in four divisions and homering for each. With Oakland in 1985, Dave sent a dead rat to a sportswriter, and the next year, after hitting 35 home runs, he became a free agent. When no one deigned to sign up the 6' 6" slugger he retired, becoming the only player with more than 30 home runs in his final season.

Only three players over the age of 40 have hit three homers in a game. Can you name these graybeard Hall of Famers?

The three are Babe Ruth, Stan Musial, and Reggie Jackson.

The Babe had his last hurrah not in Yankee pinstripes but in a Boston Braves uniform when, on May 25, 1935, he belted three homers at Pittsburgh. The final one, the last of his 714 career homers, was the first to clear the right field grandstand at Forbes Field. The clout in the seventh inning was measured at 600 feet. With that, the 40-year-old Babe lifted himself, finishing the day at four-for-four and six RBIs, and sat down in the dugout—Pittsburgh's! Ruth, who hit three homers in a game just once in the American League (May 21, 1930), was the first player to turn this hat trick in both leagues.

The oldest player to hit three round trippers in a game was Stan "The Man" Musial, who connected on July 8, 1962 at the age of 41 years and seven months. Stan hit his three in his first three times up against the Mets, and his homer the previous day came on his last at bat to beat the Mets 3–2. With four in a row leaving the yard, Stan is the oldest to accomplish that as well.

Reggie, 40 years and 4 months, clouted his three homers on September 18, 1986. It was the second time he had hit three homers in a game.

What player hit 34 homers in the same season he turned 40, a record for a player that age, and also hit more than 400 homers in his career?

Darrell Evans. The underrated third baseman played in just two All-Star Games in his 21 years, a career that started and ended with the Braves, but twice he hit 40 home runs in a season—with a 12-year gap in between.

Darrell Evans combined with two other players to become the first trio of teammates to hit 40 or more homers in the same season. What was the team, and who were the teammates?

Slugger Eddie Mathews was managing the Atlanta Braves in 1973, and he had the pleasure of filling in the names of three players on his lineup card who racked up 40 or more homers that year, the first team in history that could claim that. Darrell Evans (41), Hank Aaron (40), and Davey Johnson (43) were the threesome who would help Atlanta Fulton County Stadium acquire the nickname of "the launching pad." Johnson's next highest total was 18 in 1971 while playing for the Orioles. Despite the presence of the three sluggers, the Braves finished fifth in the NL West. Not until the Rockies in the 1990s has any team had three sluggers top the 40 home run mark.

In the home opener of 1974 Aaron cracked his record 715th homer, breaking Babe Ruth's career record. Davey Johnson was the on deck batter. Sadaharu Oh, the Japanese slugger, eventually topped both the Babe and Hank, finishing his career with

868 home runs. When Oh hit *his* 715th homer, in 1976, guess who the on deck batter was? Davey Johnson!

The three Atlanta sluggers all finished behind the 1973 National League home run leader, Willie Stargell. Which team is the only one to have the top *three* home run hitters in a season?

The fabled New York Yankees of 1927. Babe Ruth paced the team with his record 60 home runs, a mark that would last until 1961, and that was more than any other American League *team* that year. He was chased for most of the season by Gehrig, who hit 47 roundtrippers. Finishing a distant third on the team—and third in the league—was Tony Lazzeri, with 18 homers. The trio's total of 125 is exceeded only by the 143 hit in 1961 by Yankees Roger Maris, Mickey Mantle, and Bill Skowron, and by the Rockies' 130 in 1997, stroked by Larry Walker, Andres Gallaraga, and Vinny Castilla.

Back in 1884, the Chicago White Stockings (later the Cubs) had the top *four* home run hitters in the league, thanks to playing in the friendly confines of Lake Front Park. Taking advantage of the right field fence just 215 feet from home plate, the Chicago hitters combined for a record 142 dingers—all but 10 at home; the previous year a ball hit over the wall was a ground-rule double. Ned Williamson hit 27 homers—25 at home—to set a record that lasted until Babe Ruth broke it in 1919.

In 1940 the Detroit Tigers edged out the Indians and the Yankees in a tight pennant race. Paced by Rudy York's 33 home runs and Hank Greenberg's league-leading 41 homers, Detroit set a record of 17 consecutive games in which a Bengal hit a four-bagger. The mark lasted less than a year. In the middle of DiMaggio's hitting streak in 1941, the Yankees hit home runs in 25 consecutive games to set the major league record. Which team later tied their streak?

The 1941 Yankees were on their way to a pennant when they started their streak of consecutive home run games. It was finally stopped on July 1 at Yankee Stadium as 52,832 watched the pinstripers sweep a doubleheader from the Red Sox. They won the first game 7–2 but did it without any roundtrippers. The

Yankees were ahead when game two was called after five innings, but not before DiMaggio had banged out a hit to tie Willie Keeler's major league streak of 44 games. During the team's streak, DiMaggio contributed ten home runs while his teammates chipped in with an additional 30.

The Yankees' 53-year-old record of hitting a homer in 25 consecutive games lasted until 1994 when the Detroit Tigers tied it. Mickey Tettleton's upper deck blast against Toronto on June 19 made it 25 games, but the record stopped there. Cleveland's Charles Nagy beat Detroit the next day as no Tiger hits left the playing field. The Tigers hit 46 homers during the skein which began on May 25.

What is the record for hitting the most home runs in a career without a single grand slam?

In addition to being the only player to hit 60 homers in a season without leading the league, Sammy Sosa is also the player who hit the most homers before slugging a grand slam. Sosa's career charts showed a total of 207 four-baggers entering the 1998 season. By the last week of July, he had added an additional 40 to his ledger for a total of 247. On July 27, however, his streak came to an end. After 4,428 at bats, he jumped on a pitch from Willie Blair of the Diamondbacks for his 40th homer of the campaign and the first grand slam of his career. Sammy apparently liked the feeling. He belted another grand slam the very next day, just three at bats later, against Arizona's Bob Wolcott. The previous record for homers without a grand slam was 210, held by former Atlanta Brave third baseman, Bob Horner.

Roger Maris's 61st home run in 1961 was a dramatic one, coming on the last game of the season before a home crowd at Yankee Stadium. What pitcher served up the home run that broke Ruth's record?

The home run was hit on October 1st against Boston's Tracy Stallard and it broke a 0–0 deadlock between the two teams. Roger's fourth-inning solo shot, the only run of the game, was caught in the right field stands by a fan, Sal Durante, who later sold the ball for $5,000. The 1–0 victory was the Yanks' 109th of the year, one short of the then club record set by the

1927 team; the 1998 Yankee squad set a new record by winning 125 games, including 11 post-season games.

Chicago's Steve Trachsel put his name in the record books when he served up number 62 to Mark McGwire, but it was Carl Pavano we'll remember. The Expo pitcher was on the mound at Busch Stadium on September 27, 1998, when McGwire cracked his record 70th homer.

Sammy Sosa hit his 62nd off Milwaukee's Eric Plunk, and banged his 66th off Houston's Jose Lima.

Current sluggers strike out at a much greater rate than their predecessors, who seemed more intent in laying a bat on the ball. Tommy Holmes had the best single season of any slugger when, in 1945, he fanned just nine times while hitting 28 home runs—a margin of 19. Lou Gehrig struck out just 31 times in 1934 while poking 49 home runs, and Ted Kluszewski hit the same number in 1954 while striking out just 35 times.

No player has ever ended his career with more home runs than strikeouts, but one player just missed. Who is the Hall of Famer?

Joe DiMaggio. As historian Cappy Gagnon pointed out, after 12 seasons Joe D had 349 homers and just 333 strikeouts. Alas, in his final year of 1951 he had 12 home runs, but fanned 36 times, to end his career with just eight more K's than four baggers. DiMaggio had seven seasons in which he hit more home runs than he had strikeouts, the most of any player, while Yogi Berra, a notorious bad ball hitter, is next on the list with six seasons. Big Ted Kluszewski and Bill Dickey have five seasons in which they hit more homers than had strikeouts.

On the career list, Lefty O'Doul had the best ratios following DiMaggio with 113 home runs and 122 strikeouts.

The leader in clubbing home runs in extra innings is Willie Mays. The Say Hey Kid hit 22 of his 660 home runs in extra innings to lead in that category. In fact, Mays is also the only player to hit home runs in every inning from the first through the 16th frame. Which slugger is just behind Mays on the list of extra-inning home run hitters?

Jack Clark. Clark hit 18 home runs in extra innings to finish ahead of such illustrious names as Foxx, Ruth, Mantle, Aaron, Williams, and Frank Robinson. In 1990 Clark's 300th home run was his 17th in extra innings to move him one ahead of Ruth and Robinson. His 18th and last home run in extra innings came at Fenway Park on July 31, 1991, against Steve Chitren of the A's. It was Clark's third four-bagger of the game and gave the Red Sox an 11–10 win.

While Clark is second on the list to Mays in overtime clouts, he hit just over half as many home runs as Willie. Jack's 340 homers is by far the lowest on the list of extra-inning sluggers; only Willie Stargell, who hit 12 extra inning homers out of his 475, is below 500 career dingers.

One memorable home run came at the end of the 1938 season when the Cubs and the Pirates clashed at Wrigley Field. With the score tied 5–5, and the field shrouded in darkness, who hit the famous "homer in the gloamin'" to win the game?

Gabby Hartnett, who became player/manager in midseason, crashed an 0–2 pitch from Mace Brown with two out and no one on in the ninth to win the game for the Cubs over the first-place Pirates. Hartnett circled the bases as the Wrigley crowd poured onto the field to accompany Hartnett on his victory lap. Three days later Chicago clinched the pennant.

The two greatest lifetime sluggers in major league history are Babe Ruth and Hank Aaron, the man who topped Ruth's career record for home runs. Aaron broke into the majors in more ways than one in 1954, six years after Ruth had died. Aaron got the nod for the starting job after Bobby Thomson snapped his ankle sliding into third base in a spring exhibition game. Aaron went on to hit 755 home runs, with the last 22 coming while he was wearing a Brewers uniform. Which major leaguer played in Ruth's last year and Aaron's first year?

Phil Cavarretta. The popular Cavarretta signed a contract even before finishing high school at Chicago's Lane Tech. He was brought up from Peoria at the end of 1934 and was the Cubs' regular first baseman the next year. He played for the Cubs for 20 years, becoming a player/manager from 1951 to 1953. In the spring of 1954 Cavarretta was fired by Phil Wrigley

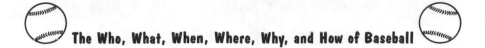

after he replied "second division" when asked by the owner "where will the Cubs finish?" He was quickly signed by the crosstown White Sox, and he hit .316 for them in 1954, Aaron's rookie year.

Who has most career homers as outfielder, Ruth or Aaron?
The Babe had 692 of his 714 home runs coming while he patrolled the outfield. Aaron hit 661 of his total (755) while playing the outfield, the rest coming when he was a designated hitter or when he was playing second or first base.

Bill Terry slugged 28 homers in the 1932 season, the same year he took over the manager's reins from an ailing John McGraw. Terry led the Giants to the pennant in 1933 and repeated in 1936 and 1937. Terry was the premier first baseman of his day, a slick fielder who could hit for average and power. He didn't make the majors until he was 26, and then he had to displace George Kelly, a future Hall of Famer, at first base. In the last game of the 1930 season, Terry went hitless against the Phillies but accomplished one feat not duplicated since. What was that?
Terry finished the game and season with a .401 average, the last National Leaguer to hit .400. The day before, Memphis Bill capped off a platinum year with a hit off Phil Collins to tie Lefty O'Doul's NL mark for most hits in a season (254). In 1930 the National League had a league *average* of .303, topped by the Giants' 20th century high of .319.

Which three major league teams, excluding Tampa Bay and Arizona, have never had a player hit 40 home runs in a season?
Not surprisingly, the three clubs who have never had a player reach the 40 home run mark have all come into existence since the expansion era began in 1961. Surprisingly, one of the three is a club which made its debut that first season. The Anaheim Angels (formerly the California Angels, formerly the Los Angeles Angels) began play that year and finished eighth in the ten-team American League. Leon Wagner clouted 28 homers in cozy Wrigley Field to lead the Halos. "Daddy Wags" smoked 37 more the next year and Bobby Bonds tied the mark 15 years

later. In January 1982, Reggie Jackson signed with California as a free agent. He proceeded to hit a league-leading 39 round-trippers to set the Angel record which has lasted 16 years.

In 1969, the Kansas City Royals joined the American League, while the Montreal Expos were added to the Senior Circuit. In the 30 years since, neither club has had a player reach the 40-homer level. The Royals' team mark was set by Steve "Bye Bye" Balboni, who hit 36 four-baggers in 1985 when Kansas City won its only World Championship. Montreal outfielder Vladimir Guerrero belted 38 for the Expos in 1998 to set their single-season standard.

Fielding

Why do players take their gloves with them between innings?
The reason is, of course, that a glove on the field might interfere with the play of the ball, but the change is a comparatively recent one. After the 1953 season, at the urging of the Cleveland front office, a rule was created requiring players to remove their gloves and other equipment from the field, both in fair and foul territory. Up till then, players would drop their gloves on the field as they headed in to hit, and catching equipment and warm-up jackets were left in warm-up areas alongside the playing field. Probably, an occasional batted ball struck a glove, or an outfielder stepped on one as he pursued a fly ball, but the only recorded occasion of equipment affecting the outcome of a game occurred in 1929, decades before the rule change. In the eighth inning of a game at Wrigley Field, the Cubs were tied 5–5 with the Reds. With the bases loaded, the Cubs' Norm McMillan hit a line drive down the left field line. Reds left fielder Evar Swanson, who was shaded towards center, saw the ball hit a gutter in foul territory near the Cubs' bullpen. But when he arrived, he couldn't find the ball. Swanson gave up his search when he saw that McMillan had circled the bases with a grand slam. At the end of the game, Cubs reliever Ken Penner picked up his warm-up jacket in the bullpen, and the missing ball rolled out of the right sleeve.

Who was the last star player to play bare-handed in the major leagues?

Bid McPhee, the great fielding second baseman, sneered at sissies who sacrificed sure-handedness for the scant protection of thin gloves. He scooped up grounders and snared line drives unflinchingly and won nine fielding titles in the 19th century. In his 15th season, the Cincinnati veteran decided finally to wear a mitt. When he opened the 1896 campaign wearing a glove for the first time, he was the object of weeks of good-natured ribbing.

Holdouts among players continue. It wasn't till 1971 that batting helmets were mandatory, replacing the hard liners in caps. Most players adapted easily, though it was not required of veteran players, and Ted Williams had complained more than ten years earlier that it interfered with his concentration. The last player to wear only a hard liner in his regular cap was Boston's Bob Montgomery, who retired in 1979. When ear flaps were added to the helmets in 1983, any player who had played in 1982 and objected to the flaps was exempted. Gary Gaetti did so and the veteran is the last player not to wear flaps.

Who invented the first catcher's mitt?

Joe Gunson. Gunson's glove, fashioned in May of 1888 and made of wire and stuffed with sheeps wool, has been displayed at the Baseball Hall of Fame since it was donated for the 1939 dedication ceremony. His design was appropriated by catcher Joe Decker and marketed by the A.J. Reach Company in 1890. "The glove was born by accident," Gunson said, recalling that he had suffered a split finger catching for the Kansas City Blues. The other catcher was out with the same injury from a foul tip and Gunson devised the glove overnight, catching a twinbill the next day. "The glove became a sensation overnight."

Who started the practice of catchers having their index finger outside the mitt?

As with many such habits, it is difficult to pinpoint who and when it came into being, but Bill Curran, in his book on baseball gloves, credits Yogi Berra. According to the story, in the mid-'50s Berra injured the index finger on his catching hand and began receiving with the finger outside the glove. He became comfortable with the feel and continued the practice even after the finger had healed. Since Berra was considered the preeminent catcher in the American League, anything he did was soon noted and others quickly followed suit. This practice soon spread to other position players and glove manufacturers jumped on the bandwagon by adding an outside finger loop.

When Bob Boone became the first player to catch 2,000 games, it was exactly 90 years after Jack Clements became the first player to catch 1,000 games. What was remarkable about Clements?

He was left-handed. Playing for St. Louis, Clements caught his 1,000th game on June 3, 1898, and also drove in the winning run over Baltimore. Clements' record was overtaken by Wilbert Robinson who in turn was topped, in 1900, by Deacon Maguire. When Dale Long caught two games in 1958, he became the first left-handed catcher in the majors since 1906. Sinister Mike Squires of the White Sox duplicated Long's feat in 1980, as did Benny Distefano of the Pirates in 1989.

Bob Boone was the only National League catcher besides Johnny Bench to win a Gold Glove in the 1970s. He hung up his mask with a record 2,225 games behind the plate only to have that mark snapped by Carlton Fisk in 1993. Fisk caught one more game than Boone, then was handed his release by the White Sox.

Of the handful of catchers in the Hall of Fame, many of them played other positions as well. Roger Bresnahan, for instance, had a 4–1 record as a pitcher, Yogi Berra played 260 games in the outfield, and Johnny Bench played more than 450 games at other positions. What Cooperstown catcher played *more* games at other positions than he did behind the plate?

Buck Ewing. The 19th century's best catcher, and one of the best all-around players, Ewing made it into the Hall of Fame in 1939. He played in a era when catchers rarely caught 100 games, and because of his athletic ability, Buck played every position including pitcher, where he compiled a 2–3 record. A .303 lifetime hitter, Ewing topped the league in homers once, and three times led catchers in assists. When he hung up his mask, Ewing had played in 1,315 games, but just 636 behind the plate.

The 1914 season was a bumpy one for infielders. Heinie Zimmerman, playing mostly third base for the Cubs, compiled a lowly .897 fielding average, while alongside him shortstop Red Corriden fumbled his way to .893 in 96 games. Two years later, A's third baseman Charlie Pick fielded just .898 while playing 108 games at third and eight in the outfield. Charlie was the last regular to field under .900, the last, that is, until 1978 when another American Leaguer did it. Who was it?

Butch Hobson. The former Alabama football star made 43 errors at third base for the Red Sox while fielding .899 in 133 games that year, but his stone hands did not stop him from later managing the team. Dick Allen kicked his way to a .908 fielding average for the Phillies in 1967, the worst in the NL since 1914, and the next year he was handed an outfielder's glove.

Triple Plays

The unassisted triple play is one of the rarest events in baseball. There have been only ten in the 20th century, and only three have occurred since the 1920s. The play is usually performed automatically, surprising both the player and baserunners. In 1992 Mickey Morandini, the Philadelphia Phillies' second baseman, caught a line drive, stepped on second base to force out the runner returning to the base, and then seemed to stumble into the unsuspecting baserunner coming from first base. Morandini was two years old when the last unassisted triple play was pulled on July 30, 1968, by Ron Hansen of the Washington Senators. And John Valentin, the Red Sox shortstop, pulled off the century's tenth unassisted triple play against Seattle on July 8, 1994.

When did the unassisted triple play happen first?
Way back in 1878, on May 8 in Providence. With runners on second and third a short fly ball was caught by center fielder Paul Hines. Both runners had been off with the hit and reached home plate. Hines kept the ball and ran to third base. When he stepped on the bag he put out both runners. His subsequent throw to second base was superfluous but got into the boxscore. It took modern era analysis to put the record straight.

What has been the shortest time span between this rare event?
In 1927 one unassisted triple play inspired another. Johnny Neun, Detroit Tigers first baseman, read in the morning paper on May 31 that Johnny Cooney, Chicago Cubs shortstop, had

made the record books the day before with a single-handed three-way putout. That afternoon, with two runners on base, Neun snared a line drive and stepped on first. The other runner was far off second base and Neun, with an unassisted triple play clearly in mind, ran over and tagged second. Cooney was also a baserunner in 1925 when Glenn Wright executed his unassisted triple play.

Who has hit into the most triple plays?

Brooks Robinson hit into four. While the Braves' Leo Foster hit into one in his first game, and the Mets' Joe Pignatano closed his career by grounding into a triple play, only the Baltimore Hall of Famer hit into four. On June 2, 1958, he hit into his first, against the Senators. Number two came against the Nats on September 10, 1964, number three the following August 18 versus Boston, and the last on August 6, 1967, against the White Sox. Another Hall of Famer, George Sisler, had set the previous mark of three in the 1920s.

Who has the only unassisted triple play executed in a World Series?

Losing 7–0 in Game 5, the 1920 Brooklyn Dodgers had two runners on base when they put on a hit-and-run play. Clarence Mitchell lined a drive over second which was snared by Cleveland's Bill Wambsganss. He stepped on second and turned to tag out Otto Miller before he could retreat to first base.

Spring Training

The rite of spring training is one the most enjoyable aspects of baseball. It is then that a fan's hopes leap the highest, when his team's rookies all look promising, and the veterans seem headed for career years. The ritual of spring training is almost as old as organized baseball and got its start in the late 1860s. Boss Tweed, of Tammany Hall fame, sent his New York Mutuals to New Orleans in 1869 to get in shape, and the champion Cincinnati Red Stockings went south the following year. Cap Anson is given credit for holding the first spring training camp, when in 1886 he brought his Chicago club to Hot Springs, Arkansas. In 1908 John McGraw took the Giants to Marlin Springs, Texas, and established the first permanent spring training camp, and other teams soon followed his example.

It was Al Lang, the father of spring baseball, who helped lure many of the teams to Florida, and by 1929, 10 of the 16 teams trained there. Since then—and only for a three-year period— one other state has been a more popular pre-season spot for teams than the Sunshine State. What state is it?

Popular might not be the right adjective, but for three years Indiana had more major league teams training there than any other state. It was WW II that caused the relocation. Baseball commissioner Landis ruled that, with the war on, spring training travel from 1943 through 45 was restricted to locations close to home. Seven teams—the Browns, Tigers, Reds, Indians, Cubs, Pirates, and White Sox—chose Indiana and trained in towns like Muncie, Terre Haute, and French Lick. The Giants and Yankees were in New Jersey, the Red Sox at Tufts College and the Braves, then in Boston, prepped at the Choate School in Connecticut. When the war ended, baseball heaved a collective sigh of relief and resumed its love affair with Florida.

Occasionally teams have ventured out of the United States for all or part of spring training. The Giants went to Havana in 1937, while the Dodgers were in Cuba for three seasons in the 1940s. The Pirates were the last team to train in Cuba, in the spring of 1953. Which team was the first to train outside the continental United States?

The Yankees have, over the years, been one of the most international of teams. In 1913 they traveled to Hamilton, Bermuda to train, the first team to be so intrepid. It was in Bermuda that the Yanks' first baseman Hal Chase fell off a bike and broke his leg. That season New York finished in seventh place, 38 games out, and chose to stick closer to home for following spring trainings. They did venture abroad again in 1946 to the Panama Canal zone in 1946 and to Puerto Rico in 1947.

One way that teams covered the expenses of spring training was by playing games against other major or minor league teams as they traveled north. This can make a team look bad, as in 1926, when the Dodgers played the Yankees 14 straight games on their way back to New York. The final score: Yankees 14, Dodgers 0. Another method of paying training costs at a minor league site was to leave behind a rookie as payment. What Hall of Famer was used this way?

In 1908 the Red Sox trained in Little Rock, Arkansas, and when they were ready to head for Boston left behind a rookie as payment. The rookie had played briefly the year before and the Sox had an understanding with the minor league team that they could purchase his contract if he played well. It was a good thing that Boston had the agreement, because the rookie hit .350 for Little Rock that year, and the Red Sox purchased his contract for $500. Tris Speaker went on play 21 more seasons in the majors, and in 1937 he and his .344 lifetime average found a home in Cooperstown.

The St. Louis Browns had the same arrangement in 1913 with the Montgomery, Alabama team, and they left a rookie as

payment, hoping perhaps he'd turn out to be another Speaker. Alas, the player was Buzzy Wares, who did make it to the majors but hit just .220 and was soon back in Montgomery.

Umpires and Rules

One boneheaded bit of baserunning occurred in the National League pennant race of 1908 and haunted the player involved even after he died. His obituary mentioned it in the first paragraph. The baserunning "error" resulted in a replay in which the Cubs trounced the Giants for the win. Who was the Giant whose bonehead play lost the pennant for New York?

Fred Merkle, the Giants' first baseman, was the baserunner. The Giants and the Cubs, along with the Pirates, won all the pennants in the NL from 1901 to 1913, and the 1908 season was the best of races. The game that resulted in putting the goat horns on Merkle actually had its roots in a play three weeks earlier. The Cubs were playing the Pirates in Pittsburg (no "h" in the spelling then) on September 4, and the game was scoreless in the tenth inning. Warren Gill was on first when the Pirates scored what appeared to be the winning run, and Gill, following the custom of the day, did not bother to touch second base before heading for the dugout. The Cubs' Johnny Evers touched second with the ball and yelled at umpire Hank O'Day that Gill was out. O'Day shook his head and the resulting appeal was denied. But awareness was aroused.

The same situation occurred three weeks later on September 23 when the Cubs and Giants were tied at 1–1 in the ninth. Merkle was on first, Harry McCormick on third, when Al Bridwell's single scored the winning run and fans flooded the field to celebrate. Merkle headed for the clubhouse without bothering to touch second, and again Evers yelled for the ball and tagged the base. This time Hank O'Day agreed and Merkle was called out.

Hank O'Day was a pitcher during his playing days, three times losing 20 games in a season, though in his last season he was 23–15. He then spent 35 years as a major league umpire, retiring in 1927 after umping in ten World Series, including the first in 1903. Who is the only man to umpire longer than O'Day?

Considered the greatest umpire in baseball history, Bill Klem had a 37-year career ending in 1941. In his first 16 consecutive years, he worked exclusively behind the plate because of his superior ability to call balls and strikes. He worked a record 18 World Series, his first coming in 1908 and the last in 1940. He even officiated a race around the bases in 1914 between a horse and speedster Hans Lobert; he called the horse a winner by a nose. Klem prided himself on never calling one wrong—then he would put his hand over his heart and add, "from here." He was elected to the Hall of Fame in 1953.

Who was an umpire in both the 1958 World Series and the 1958 NFL Championship game?

Charlie Berry. A college football All-American, Berry starred in the NFL in the mid-1920s, once leading the league in scoring. He also was a major league catcher, mostly as a reserve, ending his career in 1938 with a .267 average. Once in 1931, while catching for the Red Sox, he blocked the plate on Babe Ruth who was trying to score from third on a sacrifice fly. After the collision, Berry was still standing while Ruth was carried off the Fenway field on a stretcher and taken to a hospital. Berry became an AL umpire in 1942, and in 1958 he umped in the World Series. A few months later he was the head linesman in the famous "sudden death" championship between the Colts and the Giants.

Who is the only person to appear as an umpire and player in both the World Series and the All-Star Game?

Those with good memories will remember Lon Warneke, nicknamed "the Arkansas Hummingbird," the star pitcher for the Cubs in the early 1930s. Warneke won 100 games for Chicago before going to the Cardinals in 1937 and then returning to the Cubs in 1942. He appeared in the 1932 World Series and in the 1935 World Series, pitching the only two victories for the

Cubs. He threw four innings in the first All-Star Game in 1933, and appeared the following year for the National League and again in 1936. Warneke became an umpire in 1949, umped in the All-Star Game in 1952 and the World Series in 1954. Retiring in 1955, he ran for judge in Hot Springs, Arkansas and was elected.

Warneke pitched four one-hitters before finally humming a no-hitter against the Reds on August 30, 1941. But he never umped a no-hitter.

What ex-Cub was the umpire in the game in which Ernie Banks hit his first homer, and was umpiring when Banks hit his 500th?

A question for Cub fans, and the answer is Frank Secory. Secory played briefly in the majors with his best efforts coming in the 1945 World Series against Detroit. He was two-for-five as a pinch hitter, including a 12th inning single in Game Six to spark a rally. Secory was umpiring in a Cardinals–Cubs game on September 20, 1953 when young Ernie Banks hit his first homer, off Gerry Staley. In 1970, when Ernie hit his 500th homer, off Pat Jarvis, Secory was also umpiring the game.

Pitchers

Who is credited with developing the curveball?

Credit usually goes to William Arthur "Candy" Cummings, who first started noticing that he could throw a curveball in 1864 when he was 16. Two years later, Cummings was pitching for the Brooklyn Excelsiors Juniors and told no one, not even his catcher, of his discovery. Catchers stood well in back of the batters and took the pitches on the bounce, so Candy's slants did not cross up his batterymate. The rules of the day allowed batters to call for "high" or "low" pitches, and required that pitchers throw underhanded with no quick wrist-turns. As a curveballer, Cummings ignored the latter. Cummings gripped his curveball so hard that he wore a leather glove on his pitching hand to protect it from blisters. He once snapped off a vicious curve and broke his wrist.

In 1872 Candy's curve earned him a 33–20 record with the New York Mutuals. He won 16 games for the Hartford Blues in 1876 and that year became the first pitcher to win two games in one day. In 1877 he became a president/pitcher when he headed the International Association, the first minor league, and pitched for the Cincinnati Reds. But his skills had deteriorated and his record was just 5–14 with the Reds. He retired after 1877.

There is some support for Fred Goldsmith, who made the first recorded demonstration of the curveball on August 18, 1870, as the true inventor of the curve. The story goes that Goldsmith, embittered at not receiving credit, was found on his deathbed in 1939, clutching a faded newspaper clipping of his demonstration. It was the same year that Candy Cummings, as the inventor of the curve, was inducted into the Hall of Fame.

This Hall of Famer was one of the first elected, joining the Cooperstown elite in 1939. Continuing to fire submarine pitches in the 19th century even after the overhand throw was legalized, he was a star for Providence in the National League, completing all 73 starts in 1884 when he struck out 441 batters. Who was this outstanding 19th century hurler?

Charles Radbourn. Nicknamed "Old Hoss" for his durability, Radbourn was one of the top NL twirlers in the 1880s, and from 1882 to 1884 won 73 percent of his team's games. He won a record 49 games in 1883, and peaked the following year with 60 wins, 59 as a starter. He won 18 straight games that season. Radbourn led the Players' League in winning percentage in 1890, but in mid-1891 he dropped out of baseball having won 308 games.

Hall of Famer Hoss Radbourn is the only pitcher with over 4,000 innings who never gave up a grand slam. A handful of other outstanding pitchers have thrown 3,000 innings or more without giving up a bases-loaded gopher ball, but, except for one, all pitched at least part of their career in the dead-ball era. Which latter day Hall of Famer is the lone pitcher to throw over 3,000 innings and never give up a bases-loaded homer?

Jim Palmer. The high kicker from Baltimore won the Cy Young Award three times in his brilliant career and set an LCS record for strikeouts. Palmer won his last major league game in the 1983 World Series when he relieved Mike Flanagan in the third game, and with his decision over Steve Carlton he became the first pitcher to win World Series games in three decades. Palmer gave up a generous 303 homers in 3,948 major league innings (he also added 124 innings in post-season play without a slam), but none came with three runners on.

He did serve up one grand slam—but it happened in the minors. In July 1967, Palmer was sent to Rochester (International League) to rehabilitate from back problems, and Rochester manager Earl Weaver started the 21-year-old against Buffalo. Palmer was given a 7–0 lead, but the Bisons score five runs in the third, four coming home on a grand slam by future Hall of Famer Johnny Bench.

With the pitching distance at 50 feet, Hoss Radbourn threw a no-hitter against Cleveland on July 25, 1883, winning 8–0. Only one man has thrown a no-hitter at 50 feet and another at the current distance of 60' 6". Who was the hurler?

Ted Breitenstein. The St. Louis native thrilled the hometown fans when he tossed a no-hitter in his first major league start on October 4, 1891, against Louisville. Breitenstein won 14 games in '92, but when the pitching distance was increased to 60' 6" in 1893, he won 19 games for the weak Browns. Joining Heinie Peitz to form "the pretzel battery" in Cincinnati, he hurled his second no-hitter on April 22, 1898, against Pittsburgh.

Why is the pitching distance 60' 6"?

Unlike the 90 feet between each base, a divinely inspired distance first introduced in 1858 and not since altered, the pitching distance has bounced around more times than Al Hrabosky. Initially there was no rubber, but rather a six-foot-square pitching box, much like today's batter's box. The front line of the box was a mere 45 feet from the center of home plate, a distance made more palatable by the rule that allowed a batter to "call" his pitch, either high, low or fair (approximately waist high). In 1881 the front of the box was moved back to 50 feet, and in 1887 the box was shrunk further and batters were told to forget calling for pitches. In 1893 the pitcher's "plate" or rubber was moved to its present distance of 60' 6". It has been theorized that the proposed distance was 60' 0", but an architect or groundskeeper misread the distance as 60' 6". You make the call.

The height of the mound was set in 1903 at no higher than 15 inches, but after the 1968 season, when the pitching was so dominant, the mound was reduced to a mere 10 inches. The strike zone also shrunk that year, and the current rule, ignored by everyone including umpires, still states that it is from the letters to the knees.

The 1908 season was certainly one of the best for pennant races with a three-team fight in each league. Ed Walsh won 40

games, something no major leaguer has accomplished since, but his White Sox faltered at the end and finished in third place 1½ games out. But it was not due to any lack on his part. On October 2, in one of the great duels of all time, Walsh struck out 15 in eight innings, but lost on a passed ball. Who was the winning pitcher?

It took perfection to beat Walsh and it was there in the form of Addie Joss, who was the winner, 1–0. The Cleveland star, a 24-game winner that year, pitched a perfect no-hitter to tighten the race. Cleveland would finish with a record of 90–64. On the strength of Walsh's 40th victory, a 6–1 win over Detroit on October 5, the pennant race went down to the last day. Having been in 13 of the previous 16 games, Walsh did not start against the Tigers on October 6, and the Bengals bombed Doc White. Detroit clinched the pennant with a 90–63 record.

If Cy Young had been handing out his awards in 1908, Ed Walsh would surely have been given one. His 40 wins, as well as his winning percentage, starts, completions, innings pitched, shutouts, and strikeouts were the best. His 40–15 record accounted for 45 percent of his team's 88 victories, and no American Leaguer has ever topped that. Which National League hurler has an even higher percentage of his team's victories in one season?

Steve Carlton. With the tail-end Phils in 1972, Carlton earned—and boy, did he—one of his record four Cy Young Awards by having one of the finest seasons any pitcher has ever had. His record was 27–10, which accounted for 46 percent of his team's 59 wins. His 346 innings, 310 strikeouts and glittering 1.97 ERA were also league bests. In one stretch he compiled 15 straight wins before losing to the Braves' Phil Niekro 2–1 in 11 innings.

Who are the other six pitchers who have compiled a record of at least 10 games above .500 for teams that finished at least 20 games below .500?

Six other pitchers besides Carlton have won at least 10 more games than they've lost when their teams were at least 20 below the break-even point. Walter Johnson was the first back in 1911 when he went 25–13 for the 64–90 Senators. Ten years later, Red Faber of the White Sox was 25–15 while his team finished at 62–92. The next season, Eddie Rommel of the Athletics duplicated the feat, going 27–13 for a 65–89 team. Dutch Leonard became the second Senator hurler to accomplish the deed with a mark of 20–8 in 1939 for the 65–87 Washingtons. Carlton came along 33 years later with his incredible season. The only other National League hurler on the list is Mario Soto, who went 18–7 for the 70–92 1984 Cincinnati Reds. The last pitcher to so outclass his team was Brad Radke of the 1997 Minnesota Twins. Radke won 20 and lost only 10, while the Twins finished at 68–94.

Johnson was the only one of the seven who won more games in another season besides the one indicated. In fact, in 1913, Johnson won more than five times as many games as he lost, with a mark of 36–7—that's 29 games over .500! Washington finished second in the American League that year, with a record 26 games over .500. Even *that* pales in comparison with the record put together by Al Spalding with the Boston club of the old National Association back in 1875. That year, Spalding was 55–5, or an amazing 50 games over .500. Boston had the best record in the league with a mark of 71–8 for a winning percentage just shy of .900.

Ed Walsh, the son of "Big Ed" Walsh, also was a major league pitcher despite being the victim of rheumatic fever. He pitched four seasons in the majors, the last in 1932, but his finest moment came the following season in the PCL when he snapped a batter's 61-game hitting streak. Who was the hitter?

Joe DiMaggio. DiMaggio of course has the record for the longest hitting streak in the major leagues at 56 games, but he is also the holder of the second-longest streak ever compiled in organized baseball at 61 games. Joe Wilhoit, an outfielder for the Class A Wichita Wolves, set the longest streak of 69 games in 1919 and led the league with a .422 average before being brought up by the Red Sox.

Joltin' Joe was an 18-year-old outfielder with the San Francisco Seals when he reeled off a streak of 61 straight games in 1933 before Ed Walsh held Joe hitless in five at bats. DiMaggio ended the year with a .340 average and 169 RBIs in 187 games.

Major league hitters today strike out much more than did the players at the start of the century. The reasons for this are good topics for the hot stove league, but in fact most of the strikeout records are owned by pitchers who toiled in the last 30 years. The 10 top pitchers in strikeout ratio—strikeouts to walks—are led by Roger Clemens and Juan Marichal, who fan more than three times as many batters as they walk. Only two of the ten on this list pitched before WW I. The incomparable Christy Mathewson is one. Who is the other?

The colorful Rube Waddell, who struck out 2,316 batters and walked just 803 (a ratio of 2.88), was called by Connie Mack "the best left-hander I ever saw." Rube had a fastball that compared to that of Walter Johnson, another Hall of Famer, and led the AL in strikeouts in six straight seasons. Pitching for the A's in 1904, Waddell struck out 349, a record that stood for 69 years until Nolan Ryan broke it. (Waddell had been credited with 343, which was topped by Feller's 348 in 1946. Further digging resulted in Waddell's total increasing to 349.) In the spring of 1912, Waddell helped pile sandbags during a river flooding, and the hours of standing in the icy water affected his health. He died two years later.

Who was the last legal spitballer?

The spitball is now an illegal pitch, but it wasn't always so. Before 1920 all sorts of "foreign substances" such as Vaseline, tar or saliva were added to the baseball in an effort to affect its trajectory between mound and plate. Since no rules were in effect, oftentimes neither was subtlety, as in the case of Marty O'Toole, a pitcher from 1908 to 1914. O'Toole had the habit of holding the ball up to his face and licking it before sending it towards the plate, but he met his match in a game against the Phils in 1912. Phils' first baseman Fred Luderus stuck a tube of liniment in his pocket and rubbed the ball with it at every opportunity. Since balls stayed in the game longer back then, it took just a couple of innings before O'Toole's tongue was burning and he was forced to leave the game.

In 1920 the leagues were in a squeaky-clean mood and they outlawed any foreign substances applied to the ball. Not wanting to deprive any existing pitchers of their livelihood, provisions were made to allow each team to name two spitballers for the season, and after that, no wet ones were allowed. The following year, 17 pitchers were exempted from the spitball ban and allowed to use it for the remainder of their careers. These included such notables as Burleigh Grimes, Dick Rudolph, Bill Doak, Urban Faber, Stan Coveleski, Urban Shocker, and Jack Quinn. The 50-year-old Quinn stopped loading them up in 1933, but Burleigh Grimes lasted one more year. The 41-year-old won games for three teams in 1934 before the Yankees released him at the season's end, the last of the red hot spitballers. Grimes won 270 games in his career, 23 more than Quinn, and is in the Hall of Fame, not far from a drinking fountain.

Has any major leaguer ever pitched with both hands in a game?

The first time it happened was back in 1882 when Tony Mullane, an outstanding 19th-century pitcher, tried it against Baltimore, pitching lefty to left-handed hitters and righty to right-handers. A two-out homer in the ninth inning beat him 9–8. He tried it in 1893 and again lost. In an 1884 game, another outstanding pitcher, Larry Corcoran, tried hurling left-handed because of a painful boil on his pitching hand. But he was hit hard and replaced on the mound. The last occurrence in the 19th century was by Elton "Icebox" Chamberlain, in 1888. With an 18–6 lead after 7 innings, the Louisville right-hander pitched the final two innings left-handed, holding Kansas City scoreless.

More than 100 years later, the ambidextrous Greg Harris used both hands on September 28, 1995, in the ninth inning versus Cincinnati. Pitching for Montreal, he faced two with his normal right arm and two with his left. After Harris (right-handed) retired Reggie Sanders on a grounder, Expos manager Felipe Alou permitted him to do what he had wanted to try for 10 years. He walked Hal Morris, but remaining as a southpaw, he got Eddy Taubensee to ground out. Finally, returning the ball to his right hand, he got Bret Boone to ground out. Harris used a special six-finger glove, now on display at the Hall of Fame.

Before Harris, Bert Campaneris was the last player to pitch with both hands in a professional game, doing it in 1962 for Daytona Beach in the Florida State League. With the A's three years later, Campaneris played all nine positions against the Angels in a promotion to hype poor attendance at Kansas City. When he took the mound in the eighth inning, the first batter he faced was his cousin Jose Cardenal.

The 1971 Orioles swept to the pennant with 101 wins, the third year in a row the Birds had won 100 games. Only two other teams had accomplished that, the Philadelphia Athletics (1929–31) and the war-time Cardinals (1942–44). When Jim Palmer won his 20th game on September 26th, he joined three other 20-game winners on the O's. Who were these four 20-game winners on the 1971 Orioles?

Dave McNally (21–5), Pat Dobson (20–8), Palmer (20–9), and Mike Cuellar (20–9). McNally topped the team with 21 wins, the fourth straight year he won 20 games. But the big left-hander's finest moment probably came in the 1966 World Series when he outpitched Drysdale to win the fourth and final game 1–0.

Only one other team in history had four 20-game winners—and they finished in second place! What was the team and who were pitchers?

The 1920 White Sox, led by Eddie Cicotte, Lefty Williams, Red Faber, and Dickie Kerr, won 96 games but finished two games behind the Cleveland Indians. The Tribe's mound staff was none too shabby either with Stan Coveleski winning 24, Ray Caldwell 20, and Jim Bagby a league-leading 31 victories. For Cicotte and Williams, it was their last year. Their alleged involvement in the scandal of the 1919 World Series finally caught up with them and, along with their six fellow conspirators, the two pitchers were banned for life from organized baseball. For the veteran Cicotte, who had averaged over 20 wins the previous five seasons, it robbed him of completing a truly outstanding career. Along with Sandy Koufax, he is the only pitcher to reach 50 wins in his final two seasons.

A number of pitchers have followed a season of 20 victories with a season of 20 losses. Several of these pitchers are in the Hall of Fame, including Steve Carlton, Rube Marquard, and

60

Walter Johnson. **Who is the only pitcher to lead the league in wins and losses the same year?**

Phil Niekro in 1979. The veteran Braves knuckleballer won 21, but lost 20, the third of four years in a row he would lead the league in losses. For the third straight year he also topped the Senior Circuit in games started, completions, innings pitched, and hits allowed. His 44 starts were the most in the NL since Grover Cleveland Alexander made 44 starts in 1917. Niekro won his 20th game by beating his brother Joe, the NL's only other 20-game winner in 1979.

Since WW I, the only other pitcher besides Niekro to win and lose 20 in the same year is another knuckleballer, Wilbur Wood. In 1973 Wood topped the AL with 24 wins, the same number he had posted the previous year. But he also lost 20, one fewer than White Sox teammate Stan Bahnsen. He won 20 more in 1974, then followed with another 20 losses in 1975. In each of those four years Wood started more games than any other AL pitcher, and in 1973 he started both ends of a doubleheader against the Yankees. Wood still remains the only pitcher ever to record 20 saves in a season and win 20 the following year.

Only two pitchers in history had winning season records (15+ wins) and an ERA over 6.00. It won't be easy to recall these two.

In the year of the hitter, 1930, Guy Bush went 15–10 for the Chicago Cubs while racking up a lofty 6.20 ERA. But Bush, a solid performer who would post 176 wins in his career, was not much worse than the league ERA of 4.97. In both leagues, only Dazzy Vance had an ERA under 3.00—the Hall of Famer's was a dazzling 2.61—but with the Dodgers behind him, his record was just 17–15. Led by Bill Terry's .401, the last National Leaguer to finish a season at .400, the league combined for a batting average of .303.

Wes Ferrell, in 1938, won 13 games with the Senators and another two with the Yankees, finishing with a 15–10 record. Wes had a 5.92 ERA with the Nats, but this ballooned to a season total of 6.28 once he landed in the Stadium. Wes was one of the best-hitting pitchers ever, slamming out a record nine

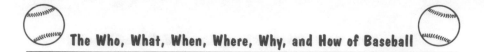

homers in the 1931 season. After his major league days were over, he won two minor league batting titles as an outfielder.

As for 20-game winners with an ERA above 5.00, that's only happened twice, once in 1930. Ray Kremer, of the Pittsburgh Pirates, went 20–12 while posting an ERA of 5.02. The other was the colorful and oft-traded Bobo Newsom, who pitched in four decades, going 20–16 for the 1938 Browns, while posting a 5.07 ERA. Newsom had six 20-game seasons—three 20-loss seasons and three 20-win campaigns—and is one of only two pitchers with 200 wins and even more losses. In his defense, the hard-luck Newsom played on some bad teams, including the Washington Senators on five different occasions. He once pitched a no-hitter for nine innings, only to lose 2–1 in the tenth.

Before 1930, seven teams had pitching staffs where five hurlers each won 15 games or more. Understandable, in an era when the pitching burden fell on smaller starting staffs. In 1930, the second place Senators had five pitchers with 15 wins. Since then, only one team has had five pitchers reach the 15-win mark in the same season. When was this?

It took nearly 60 years for it to occur again, but the Braves did it in 1998. When Denny Neagle won his 15th game in late September, he joined his four teammates Millwood, Smoltz, Maddux, and Glavine, all of whom had reached the mark. In fact, the Braves had not had five pitchers reach ten wins in the same season since 1955. After Neagle won his next start, the Braves' staff matched the 1902 Pittsburgh Pirates as the only other team to have five pitchers win 16 games or more. Neither team got to the World Series, though the Pirates had a better excuse—there wasn't one played in 1902.

In 1919, Slim Sallee won 21 games for the New York Giants, while walking only 20 batters in 227.2 innings. The talented Sallee, who had been picked up on waivers before the season, is the only 20-game winner with more wins than walks. Who is the only pitcher since then to have more wins than walks in a year?

In 1994, Bret Saberhagen won 14 games and lost 4 for the New York Mets. In 177.1 innings, Saberhagen walked just 13 batters, the same number of homers he allowed, and set a modern record of 0.7 walks per nine innings. He is just the fourth pitcher since 1900 to pitch a minimum of 150 innings and have more wins than walks. The peerless Christy Mathewson in 1913, when he won 25 games, and again in 1914 when he posted 24 wins, walked fewer batters than games won.

Several pitchers have come close to fewer walks than wins. Babe Adams missed by one in 1920, Ernie Bonham by three in 1942, and Cy Young by three in 1904. In the past 50 years, only Lamar Hoyt has come close. Hoyt won 16 and walked 20 for the White Sox in 1985.

Don Drysdale won his only Cy Young Award in 1962 when he posted a league-leading 25 wins. Teammate Sandy Koufax was the unanimous Cy Young winner in 1963, and again in 1965 and 1966. What Los Angeles pitcher took the Cy Young honors in 1964?

A bit of a trick question in that it was pitcher Dean Chance who kept the trophy in the City of Angels—but he was pitching for the Los Angeles Angels. The expansion team did not change their name from L.A. to California until the following year, and in fact were tenants in spacious Chavez Ravine when Chance posted a 20–9 record along with a glittering 1.65 ERA. He also threw 11 shutouts, including six that were 1–0 wins, and once pitched 14 shutout innings against the Yankees only to see the Angels lose 2–0 after he left the game. So Chance was the deserving winner of the lone Cy Young Award, which was given to the best pitcher in the major leagues. It was not until 1967 that each league gave a trophy to its outstanding pitcher.

Sandy Koufax was a reliever in the last game the Dodgers played before moving to Los Angeles. What later major league manager was the starter and loser in that game?

Roger Craig took the loss 2–1 as the Dodgers lost to the Phils in Philadelphia on September 29, 1957. Jim Gilliam scored the lone Dodger run. As an L.A. Dodger, Craig tied for the lead in shutouts in 1959, but as a fledgling Met in their first two seasons led the league in losses two straight years (24 in 1962, 22 in 1963). Craig later managed the San Diego Padres and the San Francisco Giants.

On May 26, 1959, Lew Burdette was the winning pitcher in one of baseball's most memorable games. That night Pittsburgh's Harvey Haddix pitched a perfect game for 12 innings, but the Pirates couldn't score off Burdette and eventually lost 1–0, in the bottom of the 13th. Which Braves slugger clouted a 13th-inning ball out of the park to end that dramatic pitchers' duel?

Joe Adcock. In the bottom of the 13th, Felix Mantilla reached first on an error by third baseman Don Hoak and was sacrificed to second. Haddix then walked Hank Aaron intentionally to pitch to Adcock, who promptly homered to end both the no-hitter and the game. Ironically, Adcock was called out for passing Aaron on the basepaths, turning his three-run homer into a one-run single, and making the final score 1–0.

Bob Gibson won only 13 games in the 1967 regular season, fourth best on the Cardinals, his subpar season due to a line drive by Roberto Clemente that broke his leg. The accident on July 15th sidelined the Cardinal star till Labor Day. But he dominated the Red Sox and tied a record by winning three times in the World Series. He won the opener 2–1, shut out the Red Sox in Game Four 6–0, then won Game Seven 7–2, while hitting a home run for good measure. He finished the series with a 1.00 ERA and 26 strikeouts in 27 innings. When the Cardinals repeated as pennant winners in 1968, Gibson won 22 games and posted a stingy 1.12 ERA. Gibson was the pacesetter in the Year of the Pitcher as both leagues combined for a sub-3.00 ERA. Who are the three pitchers in history who have season ERA better than Gibson's?

Hub Leonard is the stingiest with a 1914 ERA of 1.01, followed by Three Finger Brown (1.04) in 1906 and Walter Johnson (1.09) in 1913. Gibson's low ERA season is the only one in the top 15 since World War I. Johnson's ERA might have been lower except that two runners scored when he was replaced on the mound and went to play the outfield as the two teams fooled around in a meaningless season finale.

Ed Walsh, fifth on the all-time list for the AL with a 1.27 in 1910, actually lost 20 games that year with the White Sox, despite leading the majors in ERA.

Bob Gibson was a remarkable athlete, hitting for average and power, and winning nine consecutive Gold Glove awards. He hit two home runs in the World Series, and his 24 career dingers as a pitcher ties him with Walter Johnson for seventh place. In what other offensive category does he excel?

Stolen bases. Gibson stole 13 in 17 years for the top total by any pitcher in the last 60 years. Rip Sewell is next with 12. The all-time leader is Bill Donovan, who swiped 30 (1898–1918).

Bob Gibson was one of 14 National League pitchers to win 20 games and hit .300 in the same year. He accomplished this in 1970 when he topped the NL in wins with 23 while hitting .303. Who since Gibson pitched 20 wins while hitting .300?

Catfish Hunter in 1971. The Hall of Famer had the first of five consecutive 20-win seasons in 1971, notching a 21–11 record. He also helped his own cause by hitting a lusty .350—impressive since he was a career .226 hitter. Unless the DH rule is replaced, Hunter will remain the last AL pitcher to accomplish this mark.

Bullet Joe Bush won 26 games for the 1922 Yankees and did so without throwing a shutout. His teammates threw only seven shutouts in winning the pennant by a game over the Browns. Bullet Joe's 26 wins are the most ever by a pitcher without slipping a shutout or two into the total. Only one pitcher has ever led the league in wins without shutting out an opponent. Who was the hurler?

Ron Bryant of the San Francisco Giants had 24 wins in 1973 and racked 'em all up without a whitewash. Bryant finished just eight games that year. He slipped to 3–15 the following year following a diving board accident, was traded to the Cards, and was cut after 10 games. Bryant didn't win as many as Bush did in '22 but he topped the league in wins, which Bullet Joe just missed doing. On the other end of the record is Grover Cleveland Alexander, who whitewashed 16 opponents in 1916 on his way to 33 victories. And no one has topped that.

Another Giant, Dave Koslo of the 1949 New York team, led the National League in ERA and accomplished that without throwing a shutout. He is the only season leader in that category to not shut out an opponent.

Has any team gone through a season without recording a shutout?

Yes, the 1993 Colorado Rockies became the first team in this century to go through a season without a shutout. Before that, four teams came close.

The 1928 Boston Braves might have finished the season without a whitewash, except for rookie forkballer Ed Brandt, who tossed one on his way to leading the NL in losses. The 1977 Seattle Mariners also had a single shutout, pitched by Dave Pagan against Oakland on May 19. The 3–0 win was Pagan's only victory of the season, and the last of his career. The 1924 White Sox and the 1956 Washington Senators also recorded a single shutout each.

Twice Roger Clemens has struck out 20 batters in a nine-inning game. The Rocket's total, the highest ever in nine frames, was tied in 1998 by Cubs rookie flamethrower Kerry Wood. Four other 20th-century pitchers are one behind. In extra innings, Nolan Ryan struck out 19 three times to tie an unlikely name, Luis Tiant, who K'd 19 Twins in 10 innings in 1968. Who is the one pitcher to strike out more batters than the Rocket Man or Wood in a single game?

Back in 1962 the Washington Senators' Tom Cheney struck out 21 batters at Baltimore to set the mark. Cheney had 13 K's after nine innings but continued to pitch and struck out his 21st in the 16th frame. Bud Zipfel's homer off Dick Hall in the top of the 16th won the game for Cheney, 2–1.

Cheney suffered severe arm trouble in July of the following year and he ended his career with just 19 wins against 29 losses. But when he was healthy he was a solid pitcher, as his eight career shutouts attest.

No-Hitters

Bob Feller was a legendary fastballer at the age of 17 when he struck out eight Cardinals in a three-inning exhibition appearance. The youngster from Van Meter, Iowa, was brought up by the Indians in mid-season of 1936 and struck out 15 St. Louis Browns in his debut. In 1940 he pitched an Opening Day no-hitter, and won 27 games. He earned eight battle stars in the Navy in WW II and returned to throw two more no-hitters. The winningest pitcher in Indians history, Feller was voted baseball's greatest living right-hander in 1969. He was the first pitcher since Christy Mathewson and Walter Johnson to be elected to the Hall of Fame in his first year of eligibility. When Feller pitched his second no-hitter, in 1946, what future Hall of Famers were playing shortstop and center field?

The easy one is shortstop Lou Boudreau, who was also the manager. Boudreau would win the MVP two years later and would be elected to Cooperstown in 1970. The center fielder? Bob Lemon. Lemon was a third baseman in the minors, hitting .287, but switched to pitching and in 1946, his first season in the majors, posted a 4–5 record. He still wanted to play every day, and occasionally manager Boudreau obliged. Thus, he was in center on April 30 when Feller topped the Yankees' Bill Bevens 1–0 on a Frankie Hayes ninth inning homer. Lemon was one-for-four that afternoon, but would be elected to the Hall of Fame on the strength of his 207–128 career pitching mark.

Bob Lemon must have taken notes while playing center, for two years later he threw a no-hitter, beating the Tigers 2–0. Four years later, he pitched a near-perfect no-hitter against the Tigers, winning 2–1, as the only base runner was Vic Wertz. Wertz trotted around the bases after hitting one of his 27 homers that year. **Which pitcher had a perfect no-hitter through 26 batters, only to lose it on a home run by the 27th batter?**

One pitcher, Brian Holman, in 1990, suffered that fate. Six others—Hooks Wiltse (1908), Tommy Bridges (1932), Billy Pierce (1958), Milt Pappas (1972), Milt Wilcox (1983), and Ron Robinson (1988)—had perfect no-hitters going before they allowed the 27th batter to reach base, but only the Mariners' Holman gave up a home run. And to a former Seattle player at that, Ken Phelps. It was Phelps's only home run of the year and the last of his career. Holman then fanned Rickey Henderson.

Wiltse lost his perfecto when he hit a batter, but he ended with a 1–0 win, a no-hitter over 10 innings. Bridges, Pierce, Wilcox, and Robinson all gave up singles, while Pappas walked Larry Stahl after getting ahead 1–2 in the count.

Who is the only pitcher to miss two no-hitters in a row with two outs in the ninth inning?

Dave Stieb. The hard luck pitcher for the Blue Jays had a no-hitter through eight innings on August 24, 1985, then gave up consecutive homers to light-hitting Rudy Law and Bryan Little. In May of 1988, he threw a one-hitter against the Brewers, B.J. Surhoff being the only runner with a single. Stieb then had another close call on September 24, when, with two outs in the ninth, Julio Franco's easy grounder to Manny Lee took a bad hop over the second baseman's head for a single. Stieb settled for a 1–0 one-hit win.

In his very next start, Stieb was again one hit away from a no-hitter when Jim Traber blooped a single over Fred McGriff's head. Then, in his second start of 1989, Stieb threw a one-hitter against the Yankees, giving him three one-hitters in four starts. Finally, in 1990, Stieb did throw a no-hitter.

What pitcher was the victim of a no-hitter in his only appearance on the mound?

The player was Peaches Graham, who was brought up from the 3-I League by the Cubs (or Colts as they were then called) in 1903. Pitching in the second game of a doubleheader on September 18, Peaches gave up four runs to the Phillies in the first inning and two more in the sixth before pulling a tendon. He then left the game "at his own request" (The Philadelphia *Inquirer*), and watched the Phils' Chick Fraser throw the year's only no-hitter. Peaches appeared in another 372 major league games ending in 1912, playing every other position on the field, but his only pitching appearance was as Fraser's opponent.

The 1917 season was a strange one for no-hitters. There were two no-no's thrown in April, and on May 5 the St. Louis Browns' Ernie Koob—"Koob of Kalamazoo" (though he was born in nearby Keeler)—blanked the White Sox 1–0 on a somewhat tainted no-hitter. Koob's effort was matched the following day by teammate Bob Groom who threw another no-hitter, the sixth of a young season, against the White Sox. Groom actually threw 11 innings of no-hit ball, having gone two innings of relief in the first game and continuing for another nine innings in game two. But Groom, for the second season, still ended up losing the most games in the AL.

Four days earlier, one of the most amazing games in history occurred when, at the end of nine innings, neither pitcher had yielded a hit. Who were the two mound stars?

Fred Toney of the Reds and Chicago's Jim "Hippo" Vaughn hooked up at Weeghman Park (renamed Wrigley Field in the mid-1920s) and both were still there with no-hitters after nine innings. Vaughn was probably the better pitcher, having faced just 27 batters and striking out 10. But the wheels came off with one out in the 10th inning, as Larry Kopf singled off Hippo to break the suspense. A fly ball accounted for the second out and a line drive to Cy Williams was muffed, putting runners on first and third. Olympic star Jim Thorpe was the next batter and his little topper in front of the plate was fielded by Vaughn who scooped the ball to the catcher in a desperate attempt to get Kopf. Cincinnati had scored and it was now up to Toney. He easily retired the three Cub batters to win the only double no-hitter in history, 1–0.

Babe Ruth never threw a no-hitter, but in 1917 he combined with another pitcher to receive credit for one. Who was the other hurler and what were the curious circumstances of the game?

The other Red Sox pitcher with Ruth was Ernie Shore, who made baseball history in relief of the Bambino on June 23, 1917. Ruth was the starter at Fenway Park in the first of two games against the Washington Senators, and he quickly got into trouble with the leadoff hitter, Ray Morgan. With umpire Brick Owens behind the plate, the Babe started protesting after the first ball called. With ball four, an enraged Ruth charged off the mound to argue and took a swing at Owens. Ruth was then escorted off the field, and Shore relieved with no outs and a runner on first. Morgan was promptly erased trying to steal second and Ernie Shore then retired the next 26 batters to win 4–0 and complete the most unusual combined no-hitter in history.

Ruth was still a full-time pitcher in 1917, the ace of the Red Sox staff. He averaged more than 20 wins in the 1915–17 seasons and led the AL in several pitching categories. He totaled just nine home runs in the three years, though in the era of the dead ball this was still the most on the Red Sox. How many home runs did Ruth hit as a minor leaguer?

Just one. Pitching for Baltimore/Providence in 1914, Ruth won 22 games, briefly joining the Red Sox in July. He was sent down to Providence where, on September 5, the 19-year-old lefty beat Toronto 9–0, and hit his one and only minor league home run.

Sandy Koufax recorded a no-hitter in 1965, his fourth in successive years, and he saved the best for last. Koufax tossed a perfecto at the Cubs, allowing no base runners while winning 1–0. Sandy had to be perfect, since he was locked in a struggle with Chicago's Bob Hendley, who allowed just one hit, a bloop double in the seventh inning. That hit didn't figure in the scoring since, in the fifth, the Dodgers put together a

walk, sacrifice, stolen base, and wild pitch to plate the lone unearned run. Koufax's perfect no-hitter against Chicago on September 9 had one thing in common with his 1963 no-hitter against the Giants—the last batter was the same in each game. Who was it?

Harvey Kuenn. The former AL batting champ was in left field in the 1963 game and was a pinch hitter in the 1965 no-hitter. Both times, with two outs in the final inning, he faced Koufax, bouncing out the first time, and the second time whiffing to become Koufax's 14th strikeout victim. In the perfect game, Kuenn was the on-deck hitter when pinch hitter Joey Amalfitano, who had been the Giants' second baseman when Koufax no-hit San Francisco, struck out for the 13th K.

Koufax is the only pitcher to throw a no-hitter, win the Cy Young Award, and be named the World Series MVP all in the same year. And he did it twice. But four other players won the Cy Young Award in the same year they copped the MVP in the World Series. Who were they?

For the record, Koufax was the Cy Young winner and World Series MVP in 1963 and 1965, and in a time when just one Cy Young Award was given for both leagues. It wasn't until 1966 that each league presented its own award. Yankee pitchers Bob Turley, 21–7 in 1958, and Whitey Ford, 25–4 in 1961, won both prizes. In the 1980s Bret Saberhagen was the Cy Young winner in 1985 when he was 20–6 in the regular season. He won two World Series games to gain MVP honors that year. Saberhagen won his second Cy Young in 1989 with a 23–6 record, but the Royals did not make the Series. The last winner of both awards was Orel Hershiser in 1988 with a 23–8 record in the regular season and two wins in the World Series.

Managers

The practice of managers wearing uniforms is commonly accepted now, but it wasn't always the custom. While there were many playing managers in earlier times, bench managers often wore street clothes instead of a team uniform. Connie Mack, who started as a player/manager in 1894 and was the manager and part owner of the Philadelphia A's from 1901 to 1950, was one. From the beginning Mack sat on the bench in a suit and rarely went into the clubhouse after a game. When he retired at the age of 88 he had won more games, and lost more, than any other manager. Was he the last manager to wear street clothes?

No, Burt Shotton was. Shotton was a dependable player with the Browns when he had his first experience managing before WW I. Branch Rickey, the Browns' manager, a devout Christian, would not appear at the park on the Sabbath, so Shotton became his "Sunday manager." He skippered the Phillies from 1928 to 1933 and then became a coach. But in April 1947, Rickey's Dodgers were suddenly without a manager when Commissioner Happy Chandler suspended Leo Durocher for the season. Rickey needed a dependable manager to guide the rookie Jackie Robinson through his first year, and he called Shotton. The amiable Shotton took the team to the World Series, and stepped aside when Durocher returned. Then Durocher shocked Brooklyn fans when, in the middle of the 1948 season, he left to join the hated New York Giants. Once again, Shotton took over the Dodgers, leading them to the 1949 pennant, then losing the 1950 pennant on the last day of the season to the Phillies' Whiz Kids.

Walter O'Malley, who wrested control of the team from Rickey after the '50 season, fired Shotton on November 28, a month after Mack announced his retirement as manager. Mack's A's finished their October 3 doubleheader just minutes before the Dodgers lost to the Phillies in the 10th inning on Dick Sisler's home run. With those bits of timing, Shotton becomes the last manager to bring his street clothes to the bench.

Player/managers, once as common as triples in the major leagues, have become a rarity. In 1874 every National Association team had a player/manager and the same was almost true when the Federal League opened in 1914. Between 1901 and 1954 there were only two seasons in the American League in which no team had a playing manager. In the NL, except for 1922–23, there were playing managers every year until 1955. The 1956 season was the first year there were no player/managers in the big leagues.

Who was the last player/manager in each league?

The last player/manager in the NL was Pete Rose, in 1986, who skippered the Reds. Rose actually managed the Reds for six years ending in 1989, but for his last three seasons Pete was exclusively a bench manager.

The last player/manager in the American League was Don Kessinger, who managed the White Sox for 106 games in 1979. He resigned in early August and Tony LaRussa took over. Kessinger hit just .200 in 56 games his final year.

Who was the last player/manager to win a pennant and World Series?

Lou Boudreau with Cleveland in 1948. The shortstop/manager led the Tribe to a deadlocked finish with the Red Sox in 1948, and then Cleveland won the pennant in a one-game playoff. Cleveland then bested the Braves in the World Series. Boudreau hit .355 during the season and topped off the year by winning the AL MVP Award.

Which player/manager has the record for longevity on the job?

Joe Cronin was a player/manager for 13 seasons, and in eight of those years he was a regular. Lou Boudreau was a play-

er/manager for nine seasons with Cleveland ending in 1950, and then, two years later, got into four games as player/manager of the Red Sox.

But the record for the longest run is held by Fred Clarke, who managed for 19 years, 18 as a player. Clarke started with Louisville in the 1897 season and when the owner bought the Pirates, Clarke managed the team, beginning in 1900. Under Clarke, the Bucs won four pennants and never finished out of the first division in 14 years.

Who is the only manager to pilot a team for which he won 100 games as a pitcher, and lead them into postseason play?

Only six pitchers have managed teams for which they won 100 or more games as a pitcher. The first five—Walter Johnson (Washington Senators), Bob Shawkey (New York Yankees), Burleigh Grimes (Brooklyn Dodgers), Ted Lyons (Chicago White Sox), and Bucky Walters (Cincinnati Reds)—had varying degrees of success at the helm but never made it to the World Series. When the majors began having divisional playoffs to decide the pennant winners in 1969, it increased the number of teams who were eligible for postseason play. It was not until 1997, however, that another former pitcher pulled off the feat. Larry Dierker came out of the broadcast booth to take over the reins of the Houston Astros. He proceeded to lead the 'Stros to the playoffs in each of his first two seasons, albeit not reaching the Series. In doing so, Dierker compiled a regular-season record of 186–138, for a winning percentage of .574. In addition to being the highest percentage as a manager for any of the six, it also makes him the only one to have a higher percentage as a manager than as a pitcher for that team.

Who is the only manager to win a World Series in each league?

Sparky Anderson. Anderson managed the Cincinnati Reds Big Red Machine to World Championships in both 1975 and 1976, then won a third World Series with the Detroit Tigers in 1984.

The pugnacious, hot-tempered Roger Bresnahan was best known for his catching skills, but he broke into the major

leagues in 1897 as a pitcher. He tossed a shutout in his first game, went 4–0 and was released the following spring when he demanded more money. Back in the majors two years later, he followed John McGraw to the Giants where he hit .350 in 113 games in 1903. Traded to St. Louis in 1908, Bresnahan was the Cards' player/manager for four years, then went to Chicago where he managed the Cubs in 1915. Bresnahan's accomplishments on the field were enough to put him in the Hall of Fame, but his most notable contributions to the sport came off the field. What is the Duke of Tralee known for?

Bresnahan's greatest contributions to baseball were in the area of sports equipment. After a beaning in 1905 that left him hospitalized, Roger experimented with a batting helmet made from a cutoff leather football helmet. He was obviously ahead of his time on this one, and it did not catch on in the century's first years when even gloves were relatively new. However, in 1907 he devised shinguards for catchers, which were bulky, but later slimmed down. These were initially hooted at but soon became standard equipment. In 1908 he improved the catcher's mask by adding rolls of padding to absorb the impact of foul tips. So, while his .280 lifetime average and mediocre numbers as a manager are not well-remembered, his innovations with equipment are in use today.

Hoops and Pigskins

Frankie Baumholtz was one of a number of major leaguers to play professional basketball. Baumholtz, just 5' 10", played for the Cleveland Rebels in the NBA in 1947 and was named to the All-Star second team. Frankie hit .325 in 1952, but never made baseball's All-Star team. Eight other pro hoopsters, however, were baseball All-Stars. How many can you name?

The Milwaukee Braves' Gene Conley (Boston Celtics) was the All-Star winner in 1955 when he relieved and struck out Al Kaline, Mickey Vernon, and Al Rosen in the 12th inning. Dick Groat, the Pirates' fine shortstop of the 1950s, was another NBA player. Irv Noren (Chicago Gears of the NBL) was an All-Star in 1954 while with the Yankees, pitcher Ron Reed was the sixth man on Dave DeBusschere's Detroit Pistons in 1966–67. Reed, who pitched 19 seasons in the NL, is the only modern-era NBA player to make it to baseball's All-Star game. Other stars were Cleveland's Lou Boudreau, who captained both the basketball and baseball teams at Illinois and played for Hammond (NBL), Braves slugger George Crowe, a 6' 2" forward from Indiana Central (Dayton Rens in 1948–49), and Cardinals catcher Del Rice. Rice never went to college but played pro basketball for the pre-NBA Rochester Royals in 1945–46 and was named to the NL All-Star team in 1953. The slow-footed catcher played 17 years in the Bigs and stole just two bases. Finally, Hall of Famers Bob Gibson and Fergie Jenkins each played with the Harlem Globetrotters.

Who is the only Hall of Famer to manage a major league team and coach a pro basketball team?

Lou Boudreau. Boudreau was captain of both the baseball and basketball teams while at the University of Illinois, but when he signed an agreement to play for the Cleveland Indians after graduation, he was ruled ineligible for college ball. He played and coached for the Hammond, Indiana entry in the NBL, the predecessor of the NBA, and in 1942, at the age of 24, he was named player/manager of the Indians, the youngest ever to manage a team from the beginning of a season.

The war years thinned the talent pool for major league teams, and players that would normally have been considered too old, too young, or too marginal were pressed into uniform. A baseball uniform that is. Who was the wartime Phillie whose son wears an NBA championship ring?

Lee Riley. The 37-year-old outfielder was brought up by the Phils in 1944 but collected just one hit in 12 at bats. His son? Pat Riley, who was more successful both as a player and coach of the Lakers, Knicks, and Miami, and who has several NBA championship rings.

What NL shortstop was a college All-American in basketball?

Dick Groat, a two-time All-American at Duke, averaged over 20 points a game and was named college basketball's Player of the Year. He played just part of the 1952–53 season in the NBA, scoring 12 points a game for the Pistons, then in Ft. Wayne. But he shone at the shortstop spot, hitting .300 four times and teaming with Bill Mazeroski to provide a top-notch double play combination. In the Pirates' World Championship season of 1960, Groat was the league's MVP.

Who played for both the New York Knicks and Brooklyn Dodgers in the same year?

The answer is the organist Gladys Goodding, who also played for the New York Rangers. It was Ms. Goodding who was at the organ on September 24, 1957, the Dodgers' last night at Ebbets Field, and she sent Da Bums west with tunes like "Am I Blue?", "Thanks For the Memories," and "After You've Gone."

Who played for the Celtics, the Braves, and the Red Sox?

Gene Conley. Big Gene played basketball off-season for the Boston Celtics from 1958 through 1961 as a solid backup to center Bill Russell. Gene nearly led the Celts in fouls in two of his three seasons, as Boston won NBA championships all three years. As a rookie for the Braves—Milwaukee that is, since the team had moved to Wisconsin from Boston the previous year— Conley was third in the voting for freshman honors in 1954 and won the All-Star Game the following year. He finished his career with the Red Sox, winning a career-high 15 games in 1962.

Who compiled the highest single-season batting average of all former NFL players who have played in the major leagues?

Most single-season records of former NFL stars are held by the three most recent ones to perform in the majors. The highest batting average mark belongs to Brian Jordan, the only one currently active. Jordan batted .316 in 1998 for the Cardinals. His 100 runs scored and 178 base hits are also single-season records for NFL players. When it comes to power, however, Jordan takes a back seat to Bo Jackson. Jackson hammered 32 homers and drove in 105 runs for the Kansas City Royals in 1989. For speed, look no further than Deion Sanders, who stole 56 bases in 1997 to set the standard.

Most recent football players have been position players in the majors. To find the record for most wins in a season, you have to go all the way back to 1925 when Garland Buckeye won 13 games for the Cleveland Indians. Norm Bass's 11 victories for Kansas City in 1961 is the second-highest total ever recorded.

Since the NBA has been in existence for a shorter length of time than the NFL, there are fewer basketball stars than football stars who have played in the majors. One who starred in both, however, was Dick Groat, the National League's MVP in 1960. Groat hit .325 while leading the Pirates to the world championship that year, a mark that was duplicated by Frankie Baumholtz of the Cubs in 1952. Both are high marks for NBA players. NBA pitchers have fared better than their NFL brethren. Ron Reed holds the single-season win mark with 18 for the 1969 Atlanta Braves. Gene Conley's 15 victories for the 1962 Red Sox is the next highest total.

78

Bo Jackson was one of the most amazing athletes ever to put on a pair of spikes, and when he returned to the majors following his hip replacement, he added another chapter to his legend. Bo was drafted by the NFL but signed with the Royals and was sent to AA Memphis in 1986. When Bo finally joined Kansas City that year, he became just the second Heisman Trophy winner to play major league baseball. Who was the first?

Vic Janowicz. The Ohio State tailback won the award in 1950 as a junior but performed poorly the following year when new coach Woody Hayes installed the T-formation. The Pirates signed the Buckeye as a bonus baby but he hit just .214 in two seasons and quit baseball in 1954 to play for the Redskins. His career was ended by injuries sustained in a 1956 car accident.

Who is the only major leaguer to play in a Super Bowl?

Tommy Brown. Not to be confused with the 16-year-old shortstop who played with the Dodgers in 1944, this Tom Brown was a football and baseball star at the University of Maryland. In 1963 he went right to the majors after signing with the Washington Senators, but hit just .147 in 61 games and quit baseball for the Green Bay Packers. It was with Green Bay that Brown made his mark as a defensive back, winning rings in the first two Super Bowls.

Tampa Bay spent the NFL's number one pick on Bo Jackson in 1986. The Cleveland Browns once used their number one pick on a quarterback who turned down their offer and went to the major leagues instead. Who was this college star?

Harry Agganis. Agganis, labeled "The Golden Greek" when he was a star quarterback at Boston University, was drafted by the Browns when he was just a junior. Paul Brown tagged him "the quarterback who will succeed Otto Graham." Instead Agganis signed with the Red Sox to play baseball where BU played its home football games. Agganis led AL first basemen in assists in 1954, and had 11 homers. In June of 1955, this promising player died from a massive pulmonary embolism. He was hitting .313 at the time.

Following Agganis at quarterback at Boston University was another fine athlete who, like his predecessor, spurned football to sign a pro baseball contract. He too died tragically during the major league baseball season. Who was he?

Tommy Gastall. The young quarterback star signed a $40,000 bonus contract with the Baltimore Orioles and went directly to the majors. Used sparingly by the O's, Gastall was in his second season when on September 20, 1956, the 24-year-old catcher crashed his light plane into Chesapeake Bay. His body was found five days later.

Why was Gastall on the major league roster instead of going first to the minors?

As a way of discouraging the rich teams from signing all the young talent, a rule was instituted that required "bonus babies"—those signed for a certain amount of money—to be carried on the major league roster for two years. The reasoning was that if a team was forced to carry an unseasoned prospect, rather than a player who could help them more, a club would think twice before adding a young and rich benchwarmer. Johnny Antonelli, signed for $65,000 by the Braves in 1948, is one of the more successful examples of "bonus babies." At the other extreme, Paul Pettit, inked for $100,000 in 1951 by the Pirates, won just a single game. In 1961 the teams voted to curb bonuses and young players did not have to spend time on the major league rosters.

Who is in both the Pro Football Hall of Fame and the National Baseball Hall of Fame?

Big Cal Hubbard, an All-American tackle for tiny Centenary and Geneva colleges, who played for the 1927 NFL champion New York Giants, and then for the 1929–31 champion Green Bay Packers. Hubbard became an AL umpire the year after he retired from football, and in 1944 was the first ump to eject a pitcher (the Browns' Nels Potter) for throwing a spitball. He was supervisor of umpires for 15 years and was elected to Baseball's Hall of Fame in 1976. He is a member of both the Pro Football Hall of Fame and the College Football Hall of Fame.

What football player starred for Stanford in the 1925 Rose Bowl against the four horsemen of Notre Dame and pitched for the St. Louis Browns from 1926 to 1928?

Ernie Nevers. He was one of two football players (along with Garland Buckeye) to give up homers to Babe Ruth in 1927. The big fullback compiled just a 6–12 record for a mediocre Browns team before giving up baseball to star in the fledgling NFL. He was eventually elected to the Pro Football Hall of Fame.

Who is the only man to coach a Rose Bowl team, coach an NFL championship team, and play in the World Series?

Pro football Hall of Famer Greasy Neale. Neale played eight years in the majors, ending in 1924, and in the 1919 World Series hit .357, the highest of any Reds starters. He also coached Washington and Jefferson University in the 1922 Rose Bowl and, in 10 years as head coach of the Philadelphia Eagles, won two NFL titles.

What pro football player pinch-hit for Roger Maris, Ted Williams, and Carl Yastrzemski?

Carroll Hardy. Hardy was a defensive back for the San Francisco 49ers in 1955, and broke into the majors with the Cleveland Indians three years later. With the Red Sox in 1960, he became the only man to pinch-hit for Williams after Ted fouled a pitch off his foot and had to leave the game. In 1961 Hardy came in for Yaz in Boston. He had hit a three-run homer for Maris when the two were teammates at Cleveland.

Replacements

When a superstar leaves the lineup, his replacement has big shoes to fill. Sometimes they are filled competently with a Murcer for Mantle, who in turn had taken over for DiMaggio. If a team is lucky, the spot of a Hall of Famer is taken by another on his way to Cooperstown. In 1961 Carl Yastrzemski replaced Ted Williams in left field and upon retiring turned his glove over to Jim Rice. When Ty Cobb, then manager of the Detroit Tigers, decided he could no longer play center field on a daily basis, who stepped into his spiked shoes?

Cobb replaced himself with Heinie Manush, who promptly took up a Cobb tradition, leading the AL in batting in 1926 with a .378 average. Headed for the Baseball Hall of Fame, Manush compiled a 17-year batting average of .330, but he lagged far behind Cobb in stolen bases, netting 114 for his career against Cobb's 892.

Who was the player called "Twinkletoes," a most unlikely nickname for the man who replaced the "Sultan of Swat?"

That's the Canadian-born George Selkirk, a hustling, sharp-hitting outfielder who took over both right field and the Babe's No. 3 uniform. Over nine seasons, ended by WW II, Selkirk batted .290, had good power, and was a superb outfielder. But, he was no Babe Ruth.

When Shoeless Joe Jackson was banned from organized baseball at the end of the 1920 season, who replaced him the next season?

Although more conventionally shod, the Texan, Bibb Falk, a rookie in 1921, failed to fill Jackson's shoes. He debuted with a .285 season and built on that to a 12-season career average of .314. Falk was the ideal replacement in a non-baseball sense for the illiterate Joe Jackson. He was a University of Texas graduate, undefeated in three years of varsity pitching, and returned to his alma mater to coach Texas to 20 conference titles and two national championships.

Stolen Bases

Ty Cobb's stolen base record has been eclipsed by several modern-day speedsters, but one aspect of that total seems safe—steals of home. The Georgia Peach did it a record 54 times (or 50, depending on the record book used; since steals of home is not an official statistic, research continues on it by searching boxscores and write-ups of games), the last time coming on June 15, 1928, at the age of 41. Cobb's best year for steals of home was 1915, when he had six out of his since-eclipsed record total of 96 thefts. Six was the AL record until an AL speedster topped Cobb by swiping home seven times in a season. Who was it?

Rod Carew. Carew beat Cobb on July 16, 1969, while playing for the Twins against the White Sox, and with the steal, tied Pete Reiser for the season mark. For 1969 Carew had 19 steals. Reiser set his NL record on September 8, 1946, when he swiped three bases, including his seventh steal of home (he had nine attempts). Injury prone Pistol Pete led the majors that year in thefts with 34, despite missing 35 games.

There are more than 30 players in baseball history with 10 or more steals of home in their careers. But only three of the thieves started their careers after the 1930s. Who are they?

The talented Pete Reiser never reached double figures for thefts of home, and though he twice led the NL in steals, he had just 87 career stolen bases. In 1947 he crashed into the center field wall at Ebbets Field while chasing a fly ball, and the resulting injury was so severe he was given the last rites. According to Red Smith, no fewer than 13 times did Reiser get injured running into walls or through beanings.

Rod Carew is one of the two modern thieves of home, checking in with 17 to tie him for 14th on the all-time list. The second thief on the list is Jackie Robinson. His 19 thefts tie him for ninth on the career chart.

Who are the only two players to steal home 10 times or more and hit more than 400 home runs?

Babe Ruth and Lou Gehrig. Ruth stole home 10 times while Columbia Lou was only two steals behind Carew at 15.

How could this happen, you ask? The answer is the double steal. Except for one of the Babe's, all of Ruth's and Lou's thefts of home came on double steals, including Gehrig's first stolen base ever, on June 24, 1925. Twice Ruth was on the back end of the double steal, with Gehrig copping home, and twice Gehrig teamed with Joe DiMaggio on twin thefts. DiMaggio ended his career with just 30 stolen bases as the Yankees were reluctant to risk his legs on base stealing. The use of the double steal has declined in recent decades, but it can be effective. Lou Brock's only theft of home occurred on the front end of a successful double steal, when on May 27, 1964, he hooked up with Billy Williams.

The top base stealer among the 400-homer fraternity is Barry Bonds, who is the only player to have more than 400 homers and 400 steals.

Hall of Famer Eddie Collins is the only American Leaguer to ever steal six bases in a game. And he did it twice—in the same month! Playing for the A's on September 11, 1912, Collins took advantage of Tiger rookie catcher Brad Kocher to swipe six bases in a 9–7 Philadelphia win. Eleven days later he duplicated his feat as the A's beat the Browns 6–2. Collins swiped second base four times, third once, and stole home for good measure.

Who is the only National Leaguer to swipe six bases in a game?

Otis Nixon of the Braves became the first when he turned the trick on June 16, 1991, against the Expos. Nixon was on his way to winning the stolen bases title that year when he was suspended on September 16 for drug use. He finished four bases behind the leader Marquis Grissom. Eddie Collins had also finished second in steals (to Clyde Milan) in his 1912 season.

Who was the future Hall of Famer catching for the New York Highlanders (Yankees) in 1907 when the Washington Senators stole 13 bases off him?

Branch Rickey. Rickey made many changes in baseball, including the development of the minor league farm system while with the Cardinals and the breaking of the color barrier when he signed Jackie Robinson for the Dodgers. He was even ahead of his time when, in 1959, he attempted to expand baseball by creating a third circuit, the Continental League. The Mahatma, an innovative executive with an infallible eye for talent, had also managed both the AL and NL St. Louis teams.

Branch Rickey did not make it to Cooperstown as a player. He hit just .239, and as a sore-armed catcher he spent most of his career as a backup. On June 28, the future Hall of Famer was behind the plate for New York when the Senators took advantage of his arm to steal 13 bases in a 16–5 win. Rickey spent the rest of the season in the outfield or at first base.

Frank Isbell was a light-hitting speedy first baseman who played the first decade of the century for the White Sox. The versatile Isbell played every position including pitcher, and his .279 made him the leading hitter on the 1906 "Hitless Wonders," the World Champions. Surprisingly, several of his World Series hitting records still stand, including most hits in two consecutive games (seven) and most doubles and extra-base hits in a game (four).

In 1901, the first year of the American League, Isbell swiped 52 bases to lead the fledgling league. Another first baseman, Frank Chance of the crosstown Cubs, led the NL in steals in 1903 and 1906, and Hall of Famer George Sisler was a league leader four times. That's almost the roll call for first sackers who stole bases. Only one first baseman since then has led either league in stolen bases. Who was this thief?

Jackie Robinson. Better known as a second baseman, Robinson broke in with the Dodgers as a first baseman and in

1947 led the circuit in stolen bases with 29. The following year Gil Hodges moved from behind the plate to first base, and when Robby repeated as the stolen base champ in 1949, it was as a second baseman.

In 1988 Jose Canseco dazzled the baseball world by leading the league in homers with 42 while swiping 40 bases to become the first and only member of the "40–40" club. He also won the MVP in a landslide that year. While Canseco's 40 stolen bases was impressive, it was just the fourth best total in the AL that year. What National League player once led in homers *and* stolen bases the same year?

Chuck Klein. The Phillies' Hall of Famer was one of the most feared hitters of the late '20s and early '30s, and was right at home in tiny Baker Bowl. Klein hit .354 at home, compared to just .285 on the road, and his 44 outfield assists in 1930, a modern record, is largely due to his ability to play the caroms off the corrugated tin wall of the stadium. Klein won the MVP in 1932, the year he led the league in stolen bases with just 20 and tied for the NL high in home runs with 38. His stats at Baker Bowl that year include a .423 average, 29 homers, and 97 RBIs! Willie Mays led the league four times each in home runs and stolen bases, but he never led in both categories in the same year.

Leading the league in total bases and stolen bases is slightly less rare than the homers-and-steals combo. Chuck Klein led the NL in total bases in 1932 while leading in steals, and Ty Cobb did it five times for the Tigers. Pittsburgh's Honus Wagner was the leader in both categories three times. Who is the only other player to lead in total bases and steals in the same year?

George Stirnweiss in 1945. Snuffy was the star second baseman of the war years when hay fever and ulcers kept him out of the military service. His three hits on the last day of the 1945 season gave him the AL batting title over Tony Cuccinello, whose White Sox were rained out. Snuffy's average was .30854 to Cuccinello's .30846. Cuccinello's reward for almost winning the batting title was a pink slip from the White Sox. The 38-year-old then retired to the coaching box.

Stirnweiss was also the leader in 1945 in slugging, hits, runs, triples, total bases, and stolen bases (33). In 1944 he led the circuit in stolen bases as well as runs, hits, and triples, and missed tying Yankee teammate Johnny Lindell in total bases by just one. The other more well-known Yanks to lead in total bases include Ruth, Gehrig, DiMaggio, Mantle, and Mattingly. Mantle, certainly the fastest of the group, had only ten stolen bases in his Triple Crown year of 1956.

Hall of Fame manager Miller Huggins was a scrappy, light-hitting second baseman in his playing days. He was also slow-footed, at least in his years as player/manager for the Cardinals. In 1914 Huggins stole 32 bases but was caught 36 times, the worst percentage for anyone with more than 20 steals. Jack Fournier, a pure-hitting first baseman in the teens and twenties, is slightly better with 20 steals in 42 attempts in 1923. The marks of Huggins and Fournier were threatened in 1992. Who was the All-Star infielder with cement shoes?

Tony Fernandez. In 1992 Tony attempted 40 steals and was successful on just half of them, for the lowest steal percentage since Fournier. Fournier wasn't even the worst base stealer of the 1920s, as Larry Gardner of the Indians plodded his way to the all-time futility record with three steals in 23 attempts in 1920.

When Lou Brock hung up his spikes in 1979 he had stolen 938 bases in his 19 years. And yet just one of those steals was of home. Vic Power had just three steals in 1958, and two of those thefts were of home—both in the same game! A pitcher and teammate of Brock's stole just two bases in his 20-year career, but one of those was home plate. What hurler matched swift Lou?

Curt Simmons. On September 1, 1963, Simmons drove in a run against the Phils with a triple. With the squeeze play on, Simmons was running, but the bunt was missed and so was the tardy tag by Bob Oldis of the sliding Simmons. It took another 21 years before an NL pitcher would steal home; Pascual Perez did it for the Braves in 1984 and Rick Sutcliffe for the Cubs four years later.

Who was the last American League pitcher to steal home?

The St. Louis Browns' Harry Dorish swiped home in the fifth inning in a win against the Senators way back on June 2, 1950. Dorish, who had two doubles in the game, was on third with teammate Ray Coleman on first, when the pair teamed up on a double steal. AL pitchers made plate appearances for two more decades before the advent of the designated hitter put them on the bench, yet none matched Dorish's feat.

Who is the only player to steal two bases on one pitch?

Cardinals outfielder Dots Miller. It was during the second game of a doubleheader on August 13, 1916 that the unique play took place. On a muddy Robison Field in St. Louis, the Cards drilled 23 hits in game one to defeat the Pirates in 11 innings. The second match did not begin until 6 p.m., and when the Pirates scored eight runs in the first two innings, Pittsburgh hurried to get the game in before darkness. On the other side of the field, the Cards began to dally, hoping for the game to be called before it was an official contest. In the bottom of the second inning, the Cards' Dots Miller singled and then stole second as pitcher Al Mamaux went into a slow windup. Miller reached the base before the pitch crossed the plate and, when catcher Bill Fischer also ignored him, he continued on to third base. Two "steals" on one pitch. The Cards "stole" 11 bases as the Bucs generally ignored them, while Pittsburgh added three steals of its own for a modern record of 14. After five innings, the umps and darkness mercifully ended the game with Pittsburgh winning, 9–5. The steal rule was eventually amended so that a runner is not credited with a steal if there is defensive indifference.

Rickey Henderson, the game's greatest leadoff hitter, will hold a number of records when he eventually slows down He became the first man in the major leagues to ever steal 1,000 bases, accomplishing that feat on May 1, 1992, at Detroit. The next year Rickey added the world stolen-base record when, on June 16, he stole his 1,066th base, surpassing the record held by Japan's Yutaka Fukumoto. Henderson presented the base to Fukumoto, who was at the game. Until 1993, Rickey

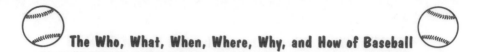

led the AL in stolen bases in every season in which he was at bat 400 times. Who finally outswiped him?

Kenny Lofton swiped 70 to lead the AL, while Henderson, bothered by a hand injury, stole 59, third best. Lofton led the previous season, one of the three seasons that Henderson went to the plate 400 times. Willie Wilson led in Rickey's rookie year, 1979, and Harold Reynolds led in 1986.

The remarkable Henderson is the all-time stolen base leader as well as being number one in home runs by a leadoff batter. He is also in the career top ten for walks and runs scored.

One player was a starter in the All-Star Game the same year he nabbed his only career stolen base. It was his only attempted theft in 1,206 games, a record skein of games in which a player was never caught stealing. Who is it?

Gus Triandos, the Baltimore Orioles' catcher from 1955 to 1962, stole his only base in a game against the Yankees in 1958. New York, with a huge lead, didn't even try to throw out the burly catcher. Triandos hit 30 home runs that year to tie Yogi Berra for most homers in a season by an AL catcher. His last homer, on September 20, was the margin of victory in Hoyt Wilhelm's first major league shutout, a 1–0 no-hitter against Don Larsen and the Yankees. Triandos' stolen base allowed him to escape breaking fellow catcher Russ Nixon's record. Nixon played in 906 games in his career without a steal, a record just surpassed in 1994 by Cecil Fielder, who is zero-for-four in career swipe attempts.

Triandos was famous for something besides his foot speed. What was the innovation he helped pioneer?

Baltimore manager Paul Richards, who possessed one of the keenest baseball minds ever, had Hoyt Wilhelm in his bullpen in the 1950s. That was the good news. The bad news was that someone had to catch Hoyt's elusive knuckler, and that was Gus Triandos and his backup Myron Ginsberg. Both of them had three passed balls in one inning within the same week in 1959, a year they let a record 49 elude them. As an aid to his beleaguered catchers, Richards came up with the idea of an extra-large mitt, one that had a circumference of 45 inches.

Whenever Wilhelm strode in from the bullpen, Triandos or Ginsberg would don the oversized mitt.

It didn't help Charlie Lau much, however, when he was splitting the catching duties with Triandos in 1962. With Wilhelm on the mound against the Red Sox on June 14, Lau tied the club and league record by allowing three passed balls in the eighth inning and added one more in the game as well. The big mitts were retired in 1965 when the rule was changed, limiting the circumference to 38 inches. This century's mark for most passed balls in an inning is four, set by the Giants Ray Katt in 1954. One guess who he was catching that day—Wilhelm.

As any baseball fan knows, the knuckleball can be as difficult for the pitcher as it is for the catcher. Another stellar knuckleballer, Phil Niekro, set a dubious mark by throwing four wild pitches in the fifth inning of an August 4, 1979 game against the Astros. The Braves' hurler threw a total of six in the contest.

Youngsters and
Old-Timers

Have any major league pitchers struck out as many batters in a game as their age?

Incredibly, two hurlers have accomplished this amazing feat.

On July 19, 1936, 17-year-old fireballing right-hander Bob Feller made his major league debut for the Cleveland Indians. Giving an indication of things to come, he fanned one batter in one inning of relief against the Washington Senators. Just over a month later, on August 23, Feller made his first big league start. He made it a memorable one by striking out 15 St. Louis Browns in a 5–1 complete game victory. Three weeks later, on September 13, he bettered that mark by fanning 17 Philadelphia Athletics to set a new American League single-game record. Still a month and ten days shy of his 18th birthday, he became the first pitcher to strike out his age in a single game. Feller almost repeated the feat two years later. On October 2, 1938, he set a new major league record by striking out 18 Detroit Tigers in a nine-inning game at the age of 19.

No one else struck out his age for more than 60 years. Then, on May 6, 1998, 20-year-old Kerry Wood of the Chicago Cubs faced the Houston Astros in only his fifth major league start. Wood proceeded to tame the Astros, allowing only one hit in the 2–0 victory. He fanned 20 batters in the contest, tying the major league record set by Roger Clemens in 1986 (at age 23), and tied by the Rocket ten years later.

When Nolan Ryan pitched in 1993 it was the 27th season the big right-hander pitched in the major leagues. This remarkable feat of longevity is a major league record, though Cap Anson also played in 27 seasons back in the 19th century, five of them in the National Association. Ryan's 27 years breaks the mark of two players, one of whom was Tommy John. Who was the other, who hung up his mask in 1912?

That would be Deacon McGuire, who toiled for 12 teams between 1884 and 1912. But McGuire appeared in just two games in 1908, and just one each in 1910 and 1912, and by then he had managed three teams in six different years. John, on the other hand, pitched in six games, his smallest total, in his rookie year of 1963. Besides the most seasons as a catcher, the Deacon holds the record as the oldest player to hit a pinch home run when he connected at the age of 43 on July 27, 1907.

Who was the oldest rookie to win 20 games?

Jim Turner was a 34-year-old rookie in 1937 when he went 20–11 for the Boston Bees (Braves). He was joined in the rotation by 30-year-old rookie teammate Lou Fette, who also won 20 games (20–10). Except for Milt Shoffner (3–1), they were the only two pitchers on the Bees to win more than they lost. Turner also took the ERA title with a 2.38 and had the most complete games in the N.L with 24. He went on to Cincy and posted a 14–7 record in 1940 with the World Champs, and in 1945, his last season, he had a league-leading ten saves for the Yankees. Turner was a pitching coach for the Yankees and Reds between 1949 and 1973.

Who was the oldest player to win his first batting title?

Charlie Gehringer was 34 years old when he won his first batting title in 1937 with a mark of .371. The quiet, sure-handed second baseman was awarded the MVP trophy that year as well. But the prize for the oldest first timer goes to Montreal's Al Oliver, who was 35 when he topped the National League in 1982 with a .331 mark.

Who is the oldest player to hit a home run?

The 46-year-old pitcher Jack Quinn cracked a homer on June 27, 1930, against the Browns and also picked up the win.

That same year the spitballer also set a record as the oldest player in a World Series, when he pitched two innings in relief. He also led the league in saves in 1932 at the age of 49, and when he hung up his spittoon at the age of 50, he had won 247 games, 109 after the age of 40.

Only one pitcher past the age of 40 has won more games than Quinn. Who was it?

When Phil Niekro's record went into the files at 121 wins after 40, he joined Quinn as the only pitcher to top 75 wins after the age of 40. Niekro's dancing knuckler was effective to the end, even if his teams were mediocre. He compiled a 17–4 mark in 1982, and in 1984, while with the Yankees, the 45-year-old compiled a 16–8 record. He was the 18th pitcher to win 300 games.

Another graybeard, who made his first pitching appearance after the age of 40, was Lena Blackburne. What is he known for?

It's not for pitching. While managing the White Sox in 1929, he made his only major league appearance when he threw to two batters on the last day of the season, not an uncommon practice back then. In other games on that same October day, 53-year-old Senators coach and resident comedian Nick Altrock went one-for-one against the Red Sox, and Browns coach Jimmie Austin, 49, and Braves coach Johnny Evers, 48, made appearances.

Blackburne made his mark in another way. Before a 1920 rule mandated that clean baseballs be used in a game, a new ball would be thrown into the game and make its way around the infield, subject to all sorts of abuse and substances before the pitcher got to hold it. After the rule change, the practice was outlawed, but umpires still needed to take the gloss off new balls. And here is where Blackburne came in. Blackburne owned a farm in New Jersey along Pennsauken Creek, a tributary of the Delaware River, and the fine grained mud of the creek was particularly good for removing the shine from new baseballs without dirtying them up. Blackburne was an A's coach in 1921 when umpires first started trying his mud. After Blackburne was let go

as the White Sox manager in 1930 he started selling his Rubbing Mud to the AL, and it was officially adopted by the league in 1938. In 1953 the NL adopted the practice, and it continues today.

Triple Crowns

Heinie Zimmerman was a backup infielder with the Cubs until 1912, when he settled in at third base and won the National League Triple Crown with 14 homers, 103 RBIs, and a .372 batting average. [Various encyclopedias and record books credit Heinie Zimmerman with 98, 99, and 103 RBIs, with one of the record books not listing him as a Triple Crown winner. The RBI was not an official statistic until 1920, which means there were no Triple Crown winners before then.]

Zimmerman broke in with the powerful Cubs in 1907, when the infield was anchored by the famed double play combination of Tinker-to-Evers-to-Chance. Who was the third baseman complementing that celebrated trio?

Harry Steinfeldt, the only one in the infield left out of the Franklin P. Adams poem and the only one left out of the Hall of Fame as well. Steinfeldt arrived by way of a trade in 1906 and led the National League that year in hits and RBIs. Not as famous as the Hall of Fame trio with whom he played, Harry has assumed a certain notoriety because of it.

Though the famed trio never did make that many double plays, the addition of Steinfeldt gave the Cubs the best fielding team in the National League. Joe Tinker led the NL in fielding percentage four times, and Johnny Evers won the MVP honors in 1914. Frank Chance, a .297 lifetime hitter, was known as "The Peerless Leader" after taking over as manager in 1905 at the age of 27. He led Chicago to four World Series between 1906 and 1910. It was in 1910 that the poem was written that immortalized the players, but ironically, it was the last year the three played together.

What other Cubs besides Zimmerman are Triple Crown winners?

Alas, he is the Cubs' *only* Triple Crown winner, though a number have won two legs of the prize. These include Cap Anson back in 1881, Wildfire Schulte (1911), Hack Wilson (1930), Swish Nicholson (1943 and 1944), Hank Sauer (1952), Ernie Banks (1958), and Andre Dawson (1987). Wilson probably came closest to winning the crown, but his .356 was not good enough in 1930, the year of the hitter.

Who is the only player to be traded right after a Triple Crown year?

The Phillies' only Triple Crown winner, Chuck Klein, won it in the Depression year of 1933 with 28 homers, 120 RBIs, and a .368 batting average. Klein also led the NL in total bases, hits, slugging, and doubles; he was second in runs, fourth in steals, and helped paint Baker Bowl in his spare time. For his efforts, Klein was sold to the Chicago Cubs a month after the season ended for $125,000 and three players. Certainly one who took advantage of the cramped and eccentric home park of the Phillies (there was a small hump in deep center field created by a railroad tunnel underneath; the outfield actually rumbled when a train went through), Klein had two solid years at Wrigley before returning to the Quaker City.

Who is the only player/manager to win the Triple Crown?

Rogers Hornsby, who took over the reins from Branch Rickey after 38 games in 1925, won the Triple Crown while managing the Cardinals to a fourth place finish. In a doubleheader split with the Braves on September 27, Hornsby hit his 38th and 39th homers of the year, along with a single, double, and triple to push his average to .403. In batting practice the next day, he fouled a ball off his foot, splitting his toenail, and sat out the last three games. The Rajah called reporters into the club house to view his bloody toe, "because some of those in the East may say I'm stallin' because I want to save my .400 average." Hornsby topped .400 for the third time in four years, hit 39 home runs and

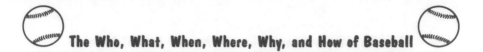

drove in 143 runs. His .756 slugging average is still the NL's best ever. The Cards finished first the following year and second in 1927 under Hornsby before the contentious star left for the Giants. Hornsby is the only National Leaguer to win the Triple Crown twice; Ted Williams is the only one in the junior circuit.

Who is the only current player to lead the league in batting, RBIs, and homers?

Andres Galarraga. The Big Cat is the only active major leaguer to be a Triple Crown winner—although not all in the same year. Galarraga won the batting crown in 1993 when he hit .370 with Colorado, and the RBI crown in 1996 when he drove in 150 runs, the most since Tommy Davis had 153 RBIs in 1962. Andres drove in 103 of the runs at Coors Field. That same year he nailed the third leg of his triple crown, belting 47 homers.

In 1967 Carl Yastrzemski hit .326 with 44 homers and 121 RBIs to win the American League Triple Crown, duplicating the feat of the Orioles' Frank Robinson the year before. Who was the last National League player to win the Triple Crown?

Joe Medwick back in 1937. Medwick hit .374 with 31 homers and 154 RBIs for the St. Louis Cardinals to win the Triple Crown. He also led all NL outfielders with a .988 fielding percentage, but St. Louis finished fourth, 15 games behind the New York Giants.

The Triple Crown for pitchers is leading the league in ERA, strikeouts, and wins. Only 15 pitchers have accomplished this and 11 of them are in the Hall of Fame. Lefty Grove did it back-to-back, in 1930 and 1931, and since then only two pitchers have reached the Triple Crown in consecutive years. Who are they?

Sandy Koufax and Roger Clemens. Koufax was the Triple Crown winner in 1963, 1965, and 1966, his final year. In 1964, he had the best ERA, winning percentage, and strikeout ratio, but he didn't lead in wins or whiffs.

Rogers Clemens is the other hurler, and the only one in history to accomplish back-to-back Triples after winning his 200th game. The Rocket Man won the Triple Crown in 1997 and 1998, just the fourth pitcher ever to do it in consecutive years.

Only seven pitchers have reached the Triple Crown twice, with Walter Johnson winning it three times and Grover Cleveland Alexander four years, three of them consecutive.

World Series

The New York Yankees hold the World Series record for the most four-game sweeps. Seven times the Bronx Bombers have humbled their National League opponents by winning all four games. The first victim was the Pittsburgh Pirates who ran into the 1927 Yankees; next was the 1928 Cardinals, followed by the 1932 and 1938 Cubs, the 1939 Reds, the 1950 Phillie Whiz Kids, and the 1998 Padres. Which team was the first to sweep the Yankees in four straight?

The 1963 Dodgers were the first to sweep the Bombers. Sandy Koufax bested Whitey Ford in the opener 5–2; that would be the most runs New York would score against the Dodgers. Los Angeles won Game Two 4–1, Bouton lost 1–0 to Drysdale, and Koufax again topped Ford 2–1 to complete the sweep.

Which team was the first to sweep their World Series opponent?

This is a tricky one. The first team to wipe out an opponent by sweeping all the games played was the fabled Miracle Braves of 1914, who demolished the overwhelming favorites, Connie Mack's Philadelphia Athletics, in four games. However, the answer to the question is the 1907 Chicago Cubs. The team of Tinker-to-Evers-to-Chance scored twice in the bottom of the ninth of the Series opener to tie the score 3–3 against the Tigers. The game went to 12 innings before it was finally called because of darkness. The Cubs then won the next four games.

What team set the record for most wins in a season and then lost in the Series?

The answer here is two teams—the 1906 Cubs and the 1954 Indians, both of which set records for season wins.

The 1906 Cubs, led by player/manager Frank Chance, finished the season at 116–36, and lost just 10 of their last 65 games. Their road record was 60–15, an .800 percentage never equaled. The Cubs, boasting a pitching staff with an ERA of 1.76, went into the only all-Chicago World Series as heavy favorites over their crosstown rival White Sox, known as "The Hitless Wonders." Still, the Cubs managed to lose in six games.

The 1954 Cleveland Indians set the since-topped AL record of 111 victories, which they accomplished in a 154-game schedule. This broke the string of five straight championships by the New York Yankees, a team that went 103–51 in '54 and still finished second behind the Tribe. The Indians then met the New York Giants, led by the timely hitting of Dusty Rhodes, and New York swept in four.

A handful of players have cracked home runs in their first World Series at bats, including such notables as Roger Maris, Mel Ott, Brooks Robinson, and Elston Howard. Even Mickey Lolich, the last pitcher to do so, hit a home run in his first Series at bat. Who is the only player to hit a home run in his *only* World Series at bat?

The Yankees' Jim Mason holds the distinction. His homer came in the seventh inning of Game Three of the '76 Series. Cincinnati pitcher Pat Zachry gave up the gopher ball.

The Brooklyn Dodgers and New York Yankees met in seven World Series. Which player played every inning of every one of those Series games?

Pee Wee Reese. The Dodger Hall of Famer was at short for Brooklyn when they took on the Bronx Bombers in 1941, 1947, 1949, 1952, 1953, 1955, and 1956. He batted .272, three points higher than his lifetime average.

Only one player has ever appeared in a World Series without playing a regular season game. Who was it?

Catcher Clyde McCullough was in the Navy in 1944 and 1945 and arrived just in time to join the Cubs, who were playing in the World Series with the Tigers. Taking advantage of a temporary rule allowing returning veterans to join their team's World Series rosters, the Cubs had veterans McCullough and pitcher Hi Bithorn on their squad. Bithorn did not appear, but McCullough pinch hit in the last game and struck out.

Nearly matching McCullough was Ken Brett, who made his pitching debut for the Series-bound Red Sox on September 27, 1967. It was his only regular-season appearance, and two weeks later he mopped up in the seventh game of the World Series against the Cardinals.

The Yankees missed a wonderful trivia opportunity after they brought up a young infielder, Chet Trail, in the last month of the 1964 season and put him on their World Series roster. But alas, the Yankees never played Trail in the seven games with the Cardinals, and when he didn't make the team the following spring Chet disappeared without ever making an appearance in a World Series or regular-season game.

Who is the only starting pitcher in a World Series not to bat ninth?

Babe Ruth. The Bambino started for the Red Sox in the fourth game of the 1917 World Series against the Cubs while batting in the sixth spot. He topped Lefty Tyler 3–2, finally giving up a run, his first after a string of 29 scoreless innings. For the Series, he had a triple in five at bats.

Which team was the only one to enter the World Series without having on its roster a .300 hitter, a 20-game winner, or a player who drove in 100 runs?

The 1973 Mets. Not only did they not even have one 80-RBI man at Shea, the Mets scored just 608 runs that year, a number exceeded by every team except San Diego. Seaver was the big winner with 19, second in the league. The Mets finished with a record of 82–79 to edge out the Pirates and the Cardinals, then beat Cincinnati to win the NL pennant.

The cry of the Boston Braves' fans in 1948 was "Spahn and Sain and pray for rain," though in fact Spahn was only slightly more effective than the next two starters, Bill Voiselle and Vern Bickford. Sain was the ace of the staff as he topped the NL in wins, innings pitched, starts, and completed games, and led the Braves into the World Series against the Indians. Sain won the first game of the Series, beating Bob Feller who allowed just two hits. The big play of the game was a pickoff attempt at second base. Pinch runner Phil Masi was ruled safe, and then scored the game's lone run on a single.

Who was the umpire who called the runner safe at second? Want another hint? He also won the Stanley Cup as coach of the Chicago Blackhawks!

Bill Stewart. Besides being a baseball umpire for 21 years, Stewart served nine years as a referee in the NHL and during the 1937–38 season coached Chicago to the NHL Championship. A few months after that, on June 15, 1938, Stewart was the ump behind the plate when Johnny Vander Meer threw his second consecutive no-hitter.

Sain's 1–0 opening game win was the third 1–0 Series game since Game Three of the 1923 World Series. What Giants outfielder won that 1923 game and also hit the first World Series home run in the new Yankee Stadium?

Casey Stengel. The 33-year-old bandy-legged Giant broke up a pitching duel in Game Three between Art Nehf and the Yankees' Sam Jones with a seventh-inning solo shot. In Game One, Stengel proved that the 20 regular-season inside-the-park homers at the Stadium had not been flukes. Casey lined a Joe Bush pitch into left center and legged it around the bases to give the Giants a dramatic 5–4 win.

Before 1948, what year had the Braves last played in the World Series?

The only other year was 1914, and it took a miracle at that. Since 1901 only the Cubs, Pirates, and Giants had won National League pennants, and in 1914 it looked like business as usual. The Giants were in first place all summer, and the Braves, after a 4–18 start, were still in last place by mid-July. Then one of the

greatest turnarounds in baseball history happened. The Mira-cle Braves put on a sensational second-half drive to take the pennant, and went into the Series as major underdogs against the powerful Athletics. Despite having just one .300 hitter dur-ing the season, the Braves pulled off the first sweep in Series history, and brought home the first—and only—championship in Boston Braves history.

One pitcher beat the New York Yankees three times in the 1957 World Series, including a 5–0 shutout in Game Seven to give the Milwaukee Braves their only World Championship. He was usually his team's second-best starting pitcher, but for 13 seasons he teamed with Hall of Famer Warren Spahn to give the Braves a devastating lefty-righty combination. Who was it?

Lew Burdette. Burdette, who started his career as a Yankee, was 17–9 with a 3.72 ERA during the 1957 regular season, but tied a record by winning Games Two, Five, and Seven in the World Series. Burdette and Spahn won 443 games as team-mates, the most ever by a lefty-righty duo.

Burdette actually pitched two shutouts in the 1957 World Series, winning a 1–0 thriller in Game Five in addition to his Game Seven triumph. What pitcher threw three shutouts in one World Series?

The New York Giants' Christy Mathewson pitched three shutouts in just six days in the 1905 World Series, blanking the Philadelphia A's 3–0 in Game One, 9–0 in Game Three, and 2–0 in Game Five. New York won the Series four games to one.

Bobby Thomson, the Staten Island Scot, closed out an amaz-ing comeback year for the 1951 Giants by smashing "The Shot Heard 'round the World." The Giants started an August 12 doubleheader against the Phils 13 games in back of the Dodgers. Sal Maglie and Al Corwin both won to launch a streak of 37 wins in 44 games and force a play-off with the Dodgers.

In the three-game play-off, the second in five years for the National League, the Giants won the opener 3–1, as Jim

Hearn bested Ralph Branca. In a sign of things to come, Branca served up home run balls to Thomson and Monte Irvin. Clem Labine shut out the Giants in Game Two, setting the stage for the dramatic Game Three. Trailing 4–2, with one out in the ninth inning and two Giants on base, Thomson smashed a three-run homer to win the game, the playoff, and the pennant for New York. Who did Branca relieve in the ninth inning?

Big Don Newcombe. Newcombe started against Maglie, but when he got into trouble in the ninth inning, manager Dressen had three pitchers, Branca, Carl Erskine, and Preacher Roe, warming up. He picked the player wearing number 13, and it was Branca who threw the gopher ball and put the final touch on the "Miracle of Coogan's Bluff."

The Giants lost the Series but they did win the opener behind surprise starter Dave Koslo and four hits by Monte Irvin. Irvin also stole home in the first inning to give the Giants a 2–0 lead. Who is the last player to steal home in the World Series?

Eleven players have stolen home in the World Series, and some of the names on the list are predictable. Ty Cobb swiped one, Bob Meusel twice pulled it off, and Jackie Robinson did it after Irvin. But the last player to swipe home in a World Series is an unlikely name, the Cardinals' Tim McCarver in 1964. McCarver, who never stole more than nine bases in any regular season, played in three World Series, but his only postseason stolen base, part of a double steal, came in his first. For the record, Robinson's was the last solo theft of home plate in the World Series.

The play-offs were instituted by the major leagues in 1969, following the expansion of the two leagues. Since then, only one player has stolen home in the play-offs. Who was the speedster?

Reggie Jackson. Mr. October had good speed and during the regular schedule swiped 228 career bases. He added one in World Series play and four in the LCS, but none was more dramatic—or costly—than his steal of home against Detroit in

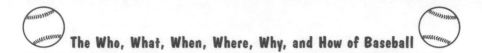

1972. Oakland was behind 1–0 when Reggie tied Game Five by swiping home and propelling the A's to a 2–1 victory. But Jackson pulled a muscle on the play and missed the World Series against the Reds. Oakland won it in seven games as Gene Tenace hit four home runs.

Fred Lindstrom broke in with the Giants in 1924 and when New York won the pennant for the fourth straight year, the rookie became the youngest player, at 18 years, 10 months, ever to start a Series game. In Game Five he had four hits against Walter Johnson, but he is best remembered for Game Seven. What happened?

With President and Mrs. Coolidge among the 32,000 fans, the Giants had a two-run lead in the eighth inning when the Senators loaded the bases. A grounder to Lindstrom at third base hit a pebble and skipped over his head to allow the tying run to score. It remained that way till the 12th inning. With one out, the Senators' Muddy Ruel lifted a foul fly, but catcher Hank Gowdy tripped on his mask and the ball fell to the ground. Ruel then doubled and Walter Johnson reached first on a Travis Jackson error. The next ball hit was a grounder to Lindstrom which again, incredibly, took a bounce over his head, and the Senators scored to win the Series.

After breaking his wrist in the final week of the 1975 season, Jim Rice could not play in either the play-offs or the World Series. Who was the Boston outfielder who rose to the occasion in Rice's absence and tied a World Series home run record?

Backup outfielder Bernie Carbo pinchhit a pair of home runs for the Red Sox in the 1975 World Series against the Reds, tying the record set by the Dodgers' Chuck Essegian in 1959. Carbo's second homer was a three-run shot in Game Six that tied the score in the bottom of the eighth and set the stage for Carlton Fisk's game-winning blast four innings later. Ironically, Carbo broke in with the Reds in 1970, hitting .310, and his 21 homers has not been surpassed by a Reds rookie since.

Which World Series winner has had the greatest drop in winning percentage from one season to the next?

After winning four pennants and three World Championships in five seasons, Philadelphia Athletics' owner/manager Connie Mack broke up the Athletics' dynasty for a variety of reasons, most of which concerned money. The upstart Federal League made overtures to several of his players, while others felt entitled to larger salaries. Above all else, Mack was a businessman. He sold and traded players left and right. The "team" he was left with finished in last place in 1915 with a mark of 43–109 for a winning percentage of .283. That was .368 lower than the .651 (99–53) mark of his pennant winners the year before.

The only other club to come within 100 points of that dubious record was the Boston Braves. Boston dropped 99 points, from .517 (78–73) in 1934 to .248 (38–115) the next season. Boston's drop, precipitous as it may have been, was only from fourth place to last. Star outfielder Wally Berger, however, did give the faithful something to cheer about. He led the National League in homers and runs batted in with totals of 34 and 130, respectively. The Braves were able to overcome his heroics, however, and finished last in the league in runs scored and earned run average. When the wreckage finally was cleared, the Braves found themselves 26 games behind the seventh-place Philadelphia Phillies!

Wayne Huizenga's dissolution of his 1997 World Champion Florida Marlins ranks third as far as percentage drops are concerned. From a 92–70 (.568) second-place finish in the NL East, the Marlins sank to 54–108 (.333) in 1998 for a drop of 235 points. That gave the Marlins the dubious distinction of losing the most games ever for a defending World Series champion. The 1991 Cincinnati Reds had held the previous record by losing 88 games a year after sweeping Oakland in the Series. Huizenga traded players with abandon, pretty much getting rid of anyone making over the major league minimum salary. The result was that Florida was forced to use a major league record 27 rookies during the course of the year.

All-Star Games

The All-Star Game was the brainchild of *Chicago Tribune* sportswriter Arch Ward, who put together the mid-summer classic as part of the Chicago Exposition in 1933. The first game was played in Comiskey Park and the opposing managers were the recently retired John McGraw for the NL, and Connie Mack, then in his 33rd year as manager of the Philadelphia Athletics. The starting center fielder for the National League in the inaugural All-Star Game was also the starter the following two years. Of the 18 starters in the 1934 classic, he is the only one *not* in the Hall of Fame. Who is he?

Braves slugger Wally Berger. If there had been a Rookie of the Year awarded in 1930, Wally Berger would have been the odds-on favorite with his .310 batting average, 38 homers, and 119 RBIs. He led the league in homers and RBIs in 1935, and was the heart of the Braves' offense for seven years. A shoulder injury in 1936 slowed him down and he was traded to the Giants. He ended his career with an even .300 average and is the all-time home run leader at Braves Field but still received just three Hall of Fame votes.

For the record, the starting lineup for the 1934 All-Star game was:

American League:		National League:	
Charlie Gehringer	2b	Frankie Frisch	2b
Heinie Manush	lf	Pie Traynor	3b
Babe Ruth	rf	Joe Medwick	lf
Lou Gehrig	1b	Kiki Cuyler	rf
Jimmie Foxx	3b	Wally Berger	cf

Al Simmons	cf	Bill Terry	1b
Joe Cronin	ss	Travis Jackson	ss
Bill Dickey	c	Gabby Hartnett	c
Lefty Gomez	p	Carl Hubbell	p

Except for the several years when there were two All-Star Games, only two players have knocked in 100 runs by the All-Star break. Who were the sluggers?

In 1935 Hank Greenberg had 101 RBI at the All-Star break (75 games)—and didn't make the team! In front of the Detroit slugger was Lou Gehrig, who played the entire game at first, while the other AL first sacker, Jimmie Foxx, played third base.

Only Juan Gonzales, with 101 ribbies in 1998, has reached the 100 RBI level by the All-Star break since. Tommy Davis had 106 RBIs by July 30, 1962, the date of the *second* All-Star Game that year, but by then Davis had played 106 games.

Hank Greenberg got his reward at the end of the 1935 season when he tied for the AL lead in homers and won the RBI title with an astonishing 51 more than Gehrig, the runner-up with 119. Greenberg won the MVP Award, and his Tigers won the World Series. While Greenberg was the first league MVP not to make it to the All-Star Game, he was not the last. The same snub befell Don Newcombe in 1956, Dave Parker in 1978, Willie Stargell in 1979, and Kirk Gibson in 1988.

In the 1937 All-Star Game, one future Hall of Famer ripped a line drive that hit another Cooperstown-bound player and virtually ended his career. Who comprised the pair?

The play came in the third inning when Dizzy Dean, miffed at allowing a home run to Gehrig, tried firing a fastball past the next hitter, Cleveland outfielder Earl Averill. Averill's line drive hit Dean on the right foot, breaking his toe. Dean, who was 12–7 at the All-Star break, would go just 1–3 for the rest of season as he would attempt to come back before the injury healed. The resulting strain on his right arm ended Dean's career, and he won just 17 more games.

Steve Garvey started out as a third baseman with a suspect arm but switched to first and became a perennial All-Star. He

was the write-in starter in the 1974 All-Star Game and won the NL's MVP that same year. He was the All-Star Game MVP in 1974 and again in 1978, two of the ten years he was an All-Star. For the Dodgers, Garvey was part of the longest-running infield of all time. Who were the other three infielders and what years did they play together?

When Garvey was switched to first, Ron Cey took over third, with Davey Lopes at second and Bill Russell at short to give the Dodgers a virtual All-Star infield from 1973 to 1981. Garvey put up Hall of Fame numbers, the smooth-fielding Russell played 18 seasons in Dodger Blue, Cey became the leading home run hitter in Los Angeles Dodger history, and Lopes set several stolen base records. When the aging Lopes was traded to Oakland in 1982, it broke up the longest running infield in history.

What year did one team provide a league's entire starting infield in the All-Star Game?

The year was 1963 and the team was the St. Louis Cardinals. Three Redbirds were voted into the starting lineup—Bill White at first, Ken Boyer at third, and veteran Dick Groat at shortstop. The Pirates' Bill Mazeroski was the fourth infielder voted to start, but he was injured, and his replacement in the lineup was the Cardinals' second baseman Julian Javier.

The 1936 All-Star Game was won by the National League 4–3, and each of the NL runs was scored by a different player from the same team: Augie Galan, Babe Herman, Frank Demaree, and Gabby Hartnett—all from the Cubs.

What team had the most players voted onto the All-Star Team?

In 1957, seven of the eight NL starters voted in were Reds, thanks to a good bit of ballot stuffing by Cincinnati fans. The lone non-Red was Stan Musial. Commissioner Ford Frick intervened and allowed just five Reds—second baseman Johnny Temple, left fielder Frank Robinson, catcher Ed Bailey, shortstop Roy McMillan, and third baseman Don Hoak to start the game. Frick eliminated three Reds—George Crowe, Gus Bell, and Wally Post—and Cincy fans threatened to sue unless they were reinstated. They weren't.

The 1939 All-Star Game in Yankee Stadium featured six starters from the home team, but they were *named* by Yankee manager Joe McCarthy, who was piloting the American Leaguers. Red Ruffing and Bill Dickey were the battery, with Joe DiMaggio in center, George Selkirk in right, Red Rolfe at third, and Joe Gordon at second. Granted, the Bombers were a virtual All-Star Team, but they were not voted into the starting lineup. Nine Yankees were named to the All-Star Team in 1939, and the Yankees again placed nine on the 1942 squad. No team has ever had more than nine All-Stars.

Three weeks after his two consecutive no-hitters in 1938, Johnny Vander Meer earned the starting assignment for the National League in the All-Star Game. Can you name the Dodger All-Star starter, the first ever for Brooklyn, who scored the game's last run?

Fiery shortstop Leo Durocher was the first Dodger to start an All-Star Game, and it paid off for the underdog National Leaguers when he got the signal to bunt with Frank McCormick on in the seventh inning. Leo the Lip laid down a perfect sacrifice and after that it was a fumble of future Hall of Famers. Jimmie Foxx, not normally a third sacker, scooped up the ball and fired to first, but second baseman Charlie Gehringer wasn't covering and the ball sailed into the outfield. Joe DiMaggio finally retrieved the ball and threw to the plate to catch McCormick, but his throw bounced over catcher Bill Dickey's head into the NL dugout for the play's second error. Meanwhile, Durocher never stopped chugging his way around the bases to score a "bunt home run."

In the 1964 All-Star Game at Shea Stadium, a National League slugger belted a three-run home run off Boston's Dick Radatz with two out in the bottom of the ninth inning to give the NL a last minute 7–4 victory. He would go on to finish the year at .274 with 31 homers and 104 RBIs and finish second in the NL MVP Award voting. Who is the player?

Philadelphia Phillies outfielder Johnny Callison. The National League trailed 4–3 entering the bottom of the ninth before Willie Mays walked, stole second, and scored the tying run on

Orlando Cepeda's bloop single. Two outs and an intentional walk then set the stage for Callison's game-winning blast. Callison's slugging during the year was not enough to offset a dramatic slide by the first place Phillies. Callison had three homers in a losing effort on September 27, when the Phillies lost their seventh in a row and dropped out of first. The losing streak stretched to ten and the team finished in a tie for second, one game back. Gene Mauch was the hapless Philadelphia skipper. He would go on to manage four different teams for a total of 26 seasons without ever winning the pennant, the all-time record for managerial futility.

Who are the two other players to hit game-ending home runs in the All-Star Game?

Ted Williams and Stan Musial. In the 1941 All-Star Game, Williams' three-run home run with two out in the bottom of the ninth gave the AL a 7–5 victory, while Musial delivered a solo home run in the bottom of the 12th to give the NL a 6–5 win in 1955.

There were 13 All-Star Games in the 1960s (several seasons featured two games) and the National League won 11 of them (with one tie). Which two players share the All-Star Game record for most times playing on the winning club?

Hall of Famers Hank Aaron and Willie Mays each played on the winning All-Star Team a record 17 times, all in the National League.

Who is the only pitcher to win an All-Star Game in each league?

Vida Blue. Blue was the starter and winner in the 1971 classic, even though he gave up three runs in his stint. The 6–4 win was the first for the American League since 1962. Ten years later, while wearing a San Francisco Giants uniform, Blue relieved Dick Ruthven and was the National League winner when Mike Schmidt hit a two-run homer in the eighth. The win was the tenth straight for the NL. Not until 1983 did the AL cash a win.

In the 1970 All-Star Game at Cincinnati's Riverfront Stadium, hometown hero Pete Rose scored the winning run in the bottom of the 12th inning in a jarring home plate collision. The play helped earn Rose the nickname "Charlie Hustle," but left the AL catcher with a separated shoulder. Cleveland Indians catcher Ray Fosse was just 23 years old when he made the All-Star Team in 1970, his first full season in the majors. He hit .307 with 18 home runs that year, but never reached either mark again during his 12-year career. Rose holds the record for the most defensive positions played as an All-Star with five. What were they?

In 16 career All-Star Games, Rose appeared at second base, left field, right field, third base, and first base. This was not unusual for Rose since he played at least 500 games at each of these positions, the only man in baseball history to play this many games at each of five spots.

Pete Rose played for seven division winners in his career: five with the Reds and two with the Phillies. What player has the most division championships on his resume?

Reggie Jackson played on a record 11 division champions in his 21-year career: five with the A's, four with the Yankees, and two with the Angels. Ironically, "Mr. October" hit just .227 in his 11 trips to the ALCS, compared to .357 in his five World Series.

Beginnings and Ends

Against which pitchers did Joe DiMaggio start and end his 56-game hitting streak?

DiMaggio started his streak in May 1941 with a modest single in four at bats against the White Sox's Eddie Smith. No one would shut out the Yankee star till July. Nine games into the streak, a hitless DiMag faced Boston's Earl Johnson in the seventh inning with two men on and first base open. Johnson declined the walk and DiMaggio laced a game-winning single. The streak almost ended in game 36 but an eighth inning single kept it alive. After 56 games, a full house at Cleveland's Municipal Stadium came out to see if Cleveland starter Al Smith could stop the slugger. Ken Keltner, the agile Tribe third baseman played deep, knowing that DiMaggio had not bunted once during his streak. Twice Joe rocketed shots down the line that Keltner stopped. Once he walked. Then in the eighth inning with the bases loaded, Jim Bagby Jr., a righty, came in to face the Yankee Clipper. DiMaggio drilled a sharp grounder to Lou Boudreau who turned it into a double play, ending the inning and the historic hitting streak.

Joe DiMaggio and Babe Ruth took the measure of every American League pitcher the sluggers faced, but two pitchers in particular hold the distinction of having given up home runs to Ruth in 1927 and hits to DiMaggio during his streak in 1941. Which two pitchers share this dubious honor?

Lefty Grove and Ted Lyons, both Hall of Famers, are the pitchers. Lyons, the White Sox's all-time wins leader, never pitched in the minors or in a World Series and spent 21 years with Chicago. He was the AL wins leader in 1927 when he gave up home run number 54 to Ruth at Yankee Stadium on September 18, 1927. By 1941 Lyons had lost his fastball and relied on a knuckleball and control to get by. Pitching primarily on Sunday, when crowds would pack Comiskey Park to see him pitch, Lyons gave up two singles to DiMaggio on July 13 to keep Joe's streak alive at 52 games.

Lefty Grove was in his third year in the majors when he gave up home run number 57, a grand slam, to Ruth on September 27 at Yankee Stadium. His last year was 1941 when, pitching for Boston, he gave up a single to DiMaggio on May 25 as DiMaggio reached game 11 in his streak. In this same game, Ted Williams raised his batting average to .400 for the first time.

Babe Ruth and Mickey Mantle, two of the greatest outfielders to wear the Yankee pinstripes, come from different eras but do have one thing in common. Both of them faced the same pitcher. Who was the hurler?

Points will be given if you say Bobo Newsom, the talkative, barrel-chested righty who toiled for eight clubs, including five stints with the Washington Senators. Newsom is one of just two pitchers to win 200 games (211) and lose even more (222). Bobo came up in 1929 and did face Ruth a number of times but never pitched to Mantle, though he pitched in the AL in 1952–53 when the Mick was playing.

But the answer is the durable Al Benton, who spent 14 years in the American League between 1934, Ruth's last season in the American League, and 1952, Mantle's second year. Benton's best season was 1941, when he went 15–6 for Boston. The following year, he relieved Spud Chandler in the All-Star Game and pitched the final five innings.

Five players pitched to both Roger Maris and Mark McGwire in the majors. All had long careers, though none served up gopher balls to both sluggers. Who was the quintet?

Nolan Ryan, Phil and Joe Niekro, Don Sutton, and Tommy John.

Nolan Ryan had a cup of coffee in 1966 but was a regular starter for the Mets in 1968. He played in both leagues through the next two decades before he settled with the Texas Rangers in 1989. Don Sutton started in the NL in 1966 and did not go to the AL until 1982. Phil Niekro started in 1964 and twenty years later moved to the American League; brother Joe started in the NL in 1967 and played for a number of teams before arriving back in the AL in 1985.

Except for his last two seasons, in 1967–68, Roger Maris was an American Leaguer, and that is where he faced Tommy John. John was in the AL from 1963 to 1971, spent six years in the NL, then went back to the AL, finally hanging it up after the 1989 season. The other four all faced Maris while he played for the Cardinals. McGwire, who broke in spectacularly in 1986, faced all five vets in the American League.

Ted Williams hit 521 home runs, including one in his last at bat, in his 19-year career that spanned four decades. The man considered by many to be the greatest hitter ever to play the game set many records, and is the only slugger to accomplish one slugging mark, hitting home runs off a father and a son. Who were the pitchers?

Thornton and Don Lee. Thornton did not reach the majors until 1933 when he was 26 years old. He struggled for four years before blossoming with the White Sox and becoming one of the top left-handed pitchers in the AL between 1937 and 1941. On September 19, 1939, rookie Ted Williams hit one of his 31 homers off Thornton. Injuries slowed Lee during the next three years, but he was still pitching at the age of 42 in 1948. Nine years later son Don, a right-hander, broke in with the Tigers and won 40 games over a nine-year span. The Splendid Splinter waited until his last month before retirement to hit a home run off Don, but on September 2, 1960, he connected during the first game of a doubleheader to become the only slugger to victimize a father and son.

When did Ted Williams slug his one inside-the-park home run?

To defend against the splendid pull hitter, Lou Boudreau, the player/manager of the Cleveland Indians, came up with the "Williams (or Boudreau) Shift." Moving from shortstop,

Boudreau played the second baseman's normal position, the second baseman moved closer to first but on the outfield grass, while the first baseman and right fielder were almost directly on the foul line. The third baseman played right on second base, while the left fielder moved in about 30 feet behind Boudreau's normal spot. Boudreau sprung the surprise shift in the second game of a doubleheader on July 14, 1946, after Williams had knocked in eight runs in the opener. Other managers quickly adopted the move.

With the shift, Boudreau dared the Splinter to bunt or punch the ball to left, something Williams stubbornly refused to do. Except once. Two months later, the Red Sox were locked in a scoreless duel with the Indians when Williams came to the plate. He punched the ball over the head of left fielder Fat Pat Seerey and chugged around the bases, sliding home with the game's lone run. Williams's one and only inside-the-park homer also clinched the pennant for the Red Sox.

Ted Williams made a pitching appearance for the Red Sox on August 24, 1940, throwing two innings against the eventual pennant winner, the Detroit Tigers. The Splinter gave up three hits in his two-inning relief stint, but just one run, and even struck out Rudy York on three pitches. The Tigers won 12–1. Who was the batterymate who caught Williams's only mound appearance and also caught Babe Ruth's last game as a pitcher?

Wearing "the tools of ignorance" was backup catcher Joe Glenn, who caught Ted Williams in his one major league pitching appearance. In Glenn's second season, 1933, he was behind the plate on October 1 when Babe Ruth pitched his final game, a 6–5 complete-game win over the Red Sox. It was Glenn's fifth game of that year and just his 11th major league game.

Relatively Speaking

Buck Ewing was the player/manager for the New York team in the Player's League in 1890 and played the following year for the New York Giants. In both those years, his brother John was a pitcher for him. John Ewing had a career losing record when he retired at the end of the 1891 season, but he went out on a high note, winning 21 games that year with an NL-best 2.27 ERA. Buck Ewing is not the *only* Hall of Fame backstop to catch his brother in the major leagues. What other pitcher-catcher brother combo includes a Hall of Famer?

Hall of Famer Rick Ferrell, who set a since-broken record for catching the most games in AL history, broke into the majors in 1929, two years after his brother, pitcher Wes, started. The two were opponents until Wes joined the Red Sox in 1934. Wes won 193 games and had a lifetime batting average of .280, just a point behind his brother's. Even though a pitcher, he hit more homers (38) than did the light-hitting Rick (28). The two were packaged in a 1937 trade to the Senators, where Rick finished his career with the daunting task of catching four knuckleballers on the 1945 team.

The brothers Mort and Walker Cooper almost qualify as an answer. Pitcher Mort won the MVP in 1942 and made the All-Star Team three times. Catcher Walker was an NL All-Star every year from 1942 to 1948 (there was no game in 1945). The two were teammates on the Cardinals and, briefly in 1947, on the Giants.

There were many brother combinations who pitched in the major leagues, some as teammates, others as opponents. But

two brothers made their first appearances in the majors three decades apart. Who were they?

Art Fowler broke in with the Reds in 1954 as a 31-year-old rookie, and toiled with mixed success for nine years, winning 54 games. In 1970 as a player/coach for Billy Martin's Denver team, Fowler saved 15 games and won 9, and then followed Martin to the majors as his pitching coach. Art's brother, Jesse, born 24 years earlier than Art, pitched for the St. Louis Cardinals back in 1924, compiling a 1–1 record. No other brothers have played in the big leagues with such a time gap between them.

Who were the first brothers to oppose each other as rookie starting pitchers?

Greg and Mike Maddux. The two rookies faced off on September 29, 1986 when the Cubs sent Greg Maddux against the Phils to face his brother Mike. Greg won, 8–3 in the first encounter between rookie brothers.

The first brothers to face each other as starting pitchers in a major league game were Jesse and Virgil Barnes. When Jesse came up to the New York Giants in 1919, his brother was already the star pitcher for the team. The two gave up Roger Hornsby's final two homers in 1922, in the same game, but it wasn't until Virgil was traded to the Braves in 1923 that the brothers faced off. They pitched against each other ten times, five as starters, with Jesse winning five and losing three.

Who was the first black father-son combo to play in the majors?

Sam, Jerry, and John Hairston. Sam Hairston, the first American-born black player signed by the White Sox, caught two games for Chicago in 1951. Working as a scout for the Sox in 1970, he signed his son Jerry, who played for the White Sox and Pirates. When Jerry was released in 1988, he was 12th on the all-time pinch hit list with 93, but he came back in 1989 and added one more. Brother John played briefly for the Chicago Cubs in 1969.

The family record for homers is held by the Bonds, who passed the Bells and the Berras in 1989. Bobby hit 332 in his

career, and son Barry is over 400. But what brothers have combined for the most homers?

The Aaron Brothers with 768. Hank hit 755 of those, while brother Tommy contributed 13. The two homered in the same game for the first time on June 12, 1962, and then homered in the same inning on July 11, one month later. Hank's was a 9th-inning grand slam to win the game. It was the first time brothers had homered in the same inning since the Waners, in 1938. On September 4, 1968, the two Aarons pulled off a double steal against the Mets. It was during this game that Mets manager Gil Hodges suffered a heart attack and missed the rest of the season.

Have any father and sons appeared in the same lineup?

That of course was the Griffeys, Ken, Sr. and Ken, Jr. The historic first occurred on August 31, 1989, when Ken, Jr. played centerfield for the Mariners and his father played left field. The Mariners signed the elder Griffey after he was waived by the Reds. They each went one-for-four in Seattle's 5–2 win over the Royals.

The Griffey pair are also the only two relatives who have connected for three homers in a game. Ken, Sr. hit three while playing for the Braves in 1986, while Ken, Jr.'s first three-homer game happened ten years later.

Can you recall the only all-brother infield or outfield?

Nineteenth century star Ed Delahanty, a Hall of Fame member, had four brothers who played in the major leagues, but only Jim was better than mediocre. While none of the brothers were teammates in the majors, in 1901, Joe, Jim, and Tom Delahanty, playing their third year together with Allentown, opened the Atlantic League season by banging out a family total of 11 hits for 20 bases.

On September 15, 1963, the Alou brothers—Felipe, Matty, and Jesus—appeared in the San Francisco outfield for one inning in a 13–5 win against the Pirates. This necessitated the "benching" of Willie Mays, and was the only time the three played in the same outfield. All three Alous were the first batters in brand new stadiums: Matty, with the Pirates, was the first batter up at the opening of Atlanta's Fulton County Stadium on April 12, 1966; brother Felipe, playing for Atlanta, was the first batter up when Busch Stadium opened in St. Louis a month later; finally, when Jack Murphy Stadium opened for business, the Astros Jesus Alou was the first batter. The Alous, not the DiMaggios, are the only trio of brothers to each collect 1,000 hits. Joe and Dom were each well over that number, but in ten years, brother Vince managed to total 959.

The all-brother infield needed two sets of brothers as the Reds doubled up on the Pirates in September, 1998, beating them 4–1. Cincinnati used a brother infield of Brett Boone at second base (zero-for-four) and his brother Aaron (one-for-two) at third base; Barry Larkin at shortstop (zero-for-three) and Stephen Larkin at first base (one-for-three). Aaron Boone's three-run homer was the winner. Stephen Larkin, a career minor leaguer with a pacemaker, had a new one installed in the previous month after his old one had a hiccup.

One pair of rookie brothers have the distinction of holding down the same infield position for the same major league team in the same season. Gene and George Freese came up as rookies with Pittsburgh in 1955. That year, Gene played 65 games at third base while his brother played another 50 at the hot corner.

Have any brothers hit back-to-back homers?

It has only happened once, and that was on September 15, 1938, when Paul and Lloyd Waner hit consecutive homers, off Cliff Melton, in a Pirates win over the Giants. It was the third time the two had homered in the same game, but the only time it was consecutive. For Lloyd, it was his last major league homer.

In the Reds-Expos game on August 15, 1998, two pairs of brothers faced each other, and three out of four went deep. Vladimir and Wilton Guerrero homered for the Expos, while Bret Boone hit a solo shot for the Reds. After Bret homered, brother Aaron followed with a strikeout.

The first time brothers on opposite teams homered in the same game was on July 19, 1933, when the Ferrell brothers did it. Red Sox catcher Rick Ferrell hit his homer off brother Wes of Cleveland in the fourth inning, and Wes answered in the same inning, hitting one off Hank Johnson. Wes wound up his career with 38 homers in 548 games, while Rick hit only 28 in 1,884 games.

The list of fathers and sons who have hit back-to-back homers is a short one, starting and ending with the Griffeys. The two hit consecutive homers in 1990.

There have been several hundred siblings who have played in the majors, and several dozen who have made it as pitchers. One pitching pair of twins, Johnny and Eddie O'Brien, arrived in the majors as infielders. Christy Mathewson won 373 games, all but the last one with the New York Giants, while his brother Henry, in his only major league decision, set a modern record by walking 14 batters in a 7–1 Giants' loss to Boston. He also hit a batter. So what brothers have won the most games?

The knuckling brothers Niekro won 539 games to just top the Perry brothers. Hall of Famer Phil Niekro won 318 games, while his younger brother Joe chipped in with 221, with the pair combining to pitch for 46 seasons. In 1973, two days after Phil pitched a no-hitter for Atlanta, the Braves purchased his brother Joe from the Tigers, only to sell him to the Astros in 1975. The two tied for the NL win lead with 21 wins in 1979, with Phil winning his 20th against Joe. But Joe got his revenge three years earlier when he hit the only home run of his 22-year major league career—and it came off his brother Phil.

The Perry brothers won 529 games between them, with Gaylord winning 314. His older brother Jim won 215 games, and they were the first 20-game winning brother combination. The Perrys both won Cy Young Awards—the only brothers to accomplish that feat—and Gaylord is the only pitcher to win the award in both leagues. Pitching for Seattle in 1982, the Ancient Mariner won his 300th game.

Who are the only pitching brothers to each throw no-hitters in the majors?

Ken and Bob Forsch. Bob, a converted infielder, threw two no-hitters in the minors and two more in the majors. He no hit the Phillies in 1978 and the Expos in 1983, while Brother Ken

threw his no-hitter at the Braves in 1979. The Forsch brothers were the third pair of siblings to win 100 games.

Books and Movies

There have been plenty of movies about major league players, teams, and managers. Two movies featured both angels and devils in them, *Damn Yankees* and *Angels in the Outfield*. The baseball musical *Take Me Out to the Ball Game* headlined Gene Kelly, Frank Sinatra, and Jules Munchin. A high note is Esther Williams singing in a swimming pool in Saratoga during the Wolves' spring training.

A few films such as *Eight Men Out, Bang the Drum Slowly, Field of Dreams,* and *The Natural* were made from marvelous books about baseball. In fact, Michael Moriarty, one of the stars in *Bang the Drum Slowly,* has good baseball genes; his grandfather was George Moriarty, a player, manager, and umpire in the majors from 1903 to 1940.

A number of biopics appeared in the late '40s and '50s, including *Fear Strikes Out,* with Tony Perkins as Jimmy Piersall; *The Babe Ruth Story,* starring William Bendix; and *The Jackie Robinson Story,* starring Jackie Robinson. Ronald Reagan played the lead in a 1952 biographical flick called *The Winning Team.* On whose life was it based?

Grover Cleveland Alexander. Frank Lovejoy (as Rogers Hornsby) and Doris Day helped out in this unconvincing turkey about Alexander's life, while Peanuts Lowrey was the major leaguer assigned to plunk the future President. The unathletic Perkins wasn't much as Piersall in *Fear Strikes Out* and the boorish Bendix was a terrible cinema Babe. Since Bendix was a natural righty, he wore a Yankee uniform with reverse lettering, and then ran to third after hitting a home run. The film was then reversed to make the Babe a left-hander.

A White Sox pitcher posted 15–5 and 15–9 records before his major league career tragically ended after a hunting accident which forced the amputation of his right leg. Wearing an artificial leg, he coached and pitched batting practice for the White Sox before coming back, eight years after his accident, to post a 18–8 record in the Class C East Texas League. A 1948 movie of his life was a box-office smash. Who was the player?

Monty Stratton, a right-hander who pitched for the White Sox from 1934 through 1938 and posted a 36–23 record by mainly throwing a trick pitch he called "The Gander." *The Stratton Story*, a fictionalized account of his life, starred Jimmy Stewart and June Allyson.

A less-known story is that of pitcher Bert Shepard, who was piloting a P–38 in WW II when the plane was shot down over Germany in May 1944. Shepard's mangled right leg was amputated below the right knee, and he was fitted with an artificial leg. The following March, the courageous Shepard went to spring training with the Washington Senators and, on August 4, threw five innings of relief and allowed just three hits. A month earlier he had defeated the Dodgers 4–3 in an exhibition game. He later pitched and played first base for the Waterbury Timers in the Colonial League.

***Eight Men Out*, John Sayles' convincing film interpretation of Eliot Asinof's marvelous book, was based on the White Sox's throwing of the 1919 World Series. Eventually, eight players were barred for life from playing in organized baseball. How many of the eight players were starters?**

Five of the eight were starters: outfielders Joe Jackson and Happy Felsch, first baseman Chick Gandil, shortstop Swede Risberg, and third baseman Buck Weaver. The other three were utility infielder Fred McMullin, who got wind of the deal and wanted in, and pitchers Lefty Williams and Eddie Cicotte, who won a league-high 29 games that year.

Bernard Malamud's classic *The Natural* was turned into one of the best baseball movies made. Whether intentionally done or not, the story, with its almost mystical overtones and classic American hero, had more than one incident that mirrored actual occurrences in major league baseball. One was the shooting of a Phillie first baseman by a deranged fan. What was the other?

The young hero of the 1952 book by the Brooklyn-born Malamud, played superbly in the movie by Robert Redford, is shot by a crazed woman fan, and it is not until years later that he plays in the majors and leads his team to victory. The shooting incident is eerily similar to one that occurred in June 1949, when Eddie Waitkus, the Phils' first baseman, was shot by Ruth Steinhagen in Chicago's Edgewater Beach Hotel. The 19-year-old girl was later placed in a mental hospital. Waitkus battled for his life, and returned to play the following season.

In 1932 a hotel room in Chicago was the scene of another shooting incident when Cubs shortstop Billy Jurges was shot in the shoulder and hand by a spurned girlfriend named Violet Popovich Valli. Jurges' wounds kept him out of the lineup for two weeks, while Ms. Valli signed a four-month contract to sing in local nightclubs. Her signature song was "What I Did for Love."

A play that echoed the climactic home run scene in the movie happened at Ebbets Field in May of 1946. At 4:25, in the night cap of two games that May 30th, the Braves' Bama Rowell cracked a second inning home run that shattered the Bulova clock high atop the right field scoreboard, and broken glass rained down on the Dodger right fielder Dixie Walker. An hour later the clock stopped.

A 1980s television movie was based on the life of Pete Gray, a courageous and skilled athlete who overcame a childhood truck accident that caused him to lose his right arm. Despite this tremendous handicap, Gray became a semipro star in the Pennsylvania coal towns where he lived, spraying hits and using his great speed. He signed in 1942, and in 1944 hit .333 for Memphis, stole 68 bases, and was named the Southern Association MVP. The St. Louis Browns, the defending champions in the AL, brought him up in 1945, but he was over-matched and hit .218 in his only season. **Which pitcher was the first and last to face one-armed Pete Gray?**

Detroit Tiger Hal Newhouser. The dominant pitcher of the mid-1940s, Prince Hal was a six-time All-Star who led the AL in wins, ERA, and strikeouts in several years. He is not the only pitcher to win an MVP, but he is the only one to win the award two years running, doing so in 1944–45, and over a five year span (1944–48) he won more games than any pitcher since 1930. Rookie Gray, who proved to be the second toughest batter in the league to strike out, faced Newhouser on April 18, and went 0–3. When Les Mueller relieved in the seventh, Gray collected his first hit.

On the last day of the season, the Browns and Tigers played with the pennant at stake. Newhouser won his 25th game as Hank Greenberg hit a grand slam in the ninth inning to win. Gray's contribution was an eighth inning fielder's choice, his last major league at bat.

Another one-armed player, Hugh Daily, had considerably more success than Gray, pitching six seasons back in the 1880s. Daily, whose left arm had been blown off in a fireworks explosion, won 23 games, including a no-hitter, for Cleveland in 1883, and recorded 28 wins and 483 strikeouts the following year.

Integration

Two Red Sox, Gene Conley and Pumpsie Green, bolted from a traffic-bound team bus after a loss at Yankee Stadium in July 1962. Conley was no doubt miffed at being lifted in the Yankee's eight-run third inning and at his teammates' failure to score a run in his last 23 innings pitched. Conley bought a plane ticket for Israel, but was refused passage because he didn't have a passport. He resurfaced three days later at his home in Massachusetts, while a tired and hungover Green rejoined the team in Washington 27 hours after his disappearance. Why is Pumpsie Green famous?

The Red Sox were the last major league team to integrate when Pumpsie Green, their first black player, appeared in a game on July 21, 1959. Pumpsie, whose brother Cornell played for the Dallas Cowboys, was joined a week later by another black player, pitcher Earl Wilson. But could the Red Sox have been the *first* team to integrate? In April 1945, under the direction of scout Hugh Duffy, the team gave tryouts to Jackie Robinson, Sam Jethroe, and Marvin Williams, though the three Negro League players never heard from the team again. Six months later the Dodgers signed Robinson, and in 1950 Jethroe became the Boston Braves' first black player. Williams continued in the Negro Leagues and later had some outstanding seasons in the Pacific Coast League and Texas League.

When Jackie Robinson opened the 1947 season with the Dodgers, it officially brought integration to 20th century major league baseball. Not since the 1880s, when Moses Walk-

er played for Toledo of the American Association, then considered a major league, had the majors seen a black American player. In the 1920s, two dark-skinned Cubans, Jack Calvo and Jose Acosta, played in the major leagues as well as the Negro Leagues. But it was made clear that these were foreigners, exotic of habit, speaking in strangely accented English, and not native born.

Robinson was soon joined by Larry Doby, the first black player in the American League, who started for the Indians in 1947, a few months after Robinson opened the season. But who followed Robinson as the *second* black player in the National League?

Dan Bankhead. Brooklyn signed Bankhead from the Negro League Memphis Red Sox roster, and the veteran made his first appearance for the Dodgers on August 26, 1947. The Pirates rocked the major's first black pitcher for 10 hits in 3⅓ innings, but Bankhead did join a small group of major leaguers by hitting a home run in his first at bat. Bankhead got into four games in 1947, won 20 in each of his next two seasons in the minors, and then pitched for Brooklyn in 1950–51.

Which National League team was the last to integrate, and who was the player?

The Philadelphia Phillies in 1957 became the last team to have an African American player when John Irvin Kennedy appeared in an April 22 game as a pinch runner. The former Birmingham Black Baron player appeared in just five games and went hitless. Five days earlier, on Opening Night, the Phils used their first black player, the Cuban-born Chico Fernandez, who had been acquired from the Dodgers. Fernandez later became the second black player on the Tigers.

The integration of the major leagues was the death knell for the Negro Leagues, though the interment took a few years. The year 1955 was the last one for teams like the Memphis Red Sox, Detroit Stars, Kansas City Monarchs, and the Birmingham Black Barons. The Indianapolis Clowns struggled on for several years as an exhibition team, but the semblance of league play was finished. A number of players from that last

season did make it to the majors as late as the 1960s, but what Negro League veteran from that final year was the last to make it to the majors?

The answer, admittedly a curve, is the ageless Satchel Paige who was toiling for the Kansas City Monarchs in 1955 when the team folded. Ten years later, on September 25, 1965, The Ancient One was brought back for a farewell hurrah by the Kansas City A's. At the age of 59 or so, he pitched three innings against the Red Sox and yielded just a hit, a double to Carl Yastrzemski. The Sox then jumped on reliever Don Mossi to win 5–2.

Paige, of course, was not making his first appearance in the majors in 1965. As Dick Clark and Larry Lester point out in their book on the Negro Leagues, the *last* Negro League player to be a rookie in the majors was Indianapolis Clowns second baseman George Smith, who appeared for the Tigers on August 4, 1963. Smith played for Indianapolis in 1956–57, and then signed with Durham in the Carolina League. The good-fielding Smith played four years in the majors, hitting .205.

The last Negro League player in the majors was none other than Hank Aaron, whose final season was 1976. Aaron started as an infielder with the Indianapolis Clowns in 1952 before signing with the Braves.

Who Played For...?

Who was the only player to play for the Boston Braves, the Milwaukee Braves, and the Atlanta Braves?

No, it was not Hank Aaron, who made his first appearance in a Braves uniform in 1954, the Braves' second year in the Brew City. The other half of the greatest slugging duo in history was Eddie Mathews, who combined with Hammerin' Hank to hit 863 homers as teammates. Mathews hit 25 homers his first year up with the Braves in 1952, which was the franchise's last season in Beantown before moving to Milwaukee. Mathews hit 32 homers in 1965, the Braves' last season in Milwaukee, but slumped to 16 homers the next year in Atlanta and left for Houston.

Who was the only pitcher to *beat* the Boston Braves, the Milwaukee Braves and the Atlanta Braves?

Robin Roberts. The Hall of Famer was 12–6 against the Boston Braves and 21–24 against the Milwaukee Braves, all coming while he was with the Phils. In 1965 Roberts went 1–0 against the Atlanta team after returning to the National League with Houston.

Beginning in 1954, Aaron was a star for the Milwaukee Braves, and when the franchise moved to Atlanta, he continued his slugging ways. When his home runs dropped to 20 in 1974, he and the Braves parted company, and Hank returned to Milwaukee as a Brewer for the last two seasons of his

career. Only one other player wore the uniform of both the Milwaukee Braves and the Milwaukee Brewers. Who was it?

Phil Roof. The well-traveled veteran catcher began his career with the Braves in 1961 and was acquired by the Brewers before the start of 1970, their first season in Milwaukee after departing Seattle. He played a career-high 127 games for the A's in 1966.

Who is the only player to play for the Seattle Pilots and the Seattle Mariners?

Diego Segui. Segui broke in with the A's in 1962 and in 1969, the Pilots' only season in the majors, was the primary reliever for them. When the Pilots abruptly moved to Milwaukee in 1970, Seattle threatened to sue major league baseball unless another franchise was awarded to the city. Major league baseball complied, and in 1977 the new Seattle Mariners took the field. Segui, then in his 15th year, was among them, though the righty didn't help them much. He finished his final season at 0–7.

Who is the only Hall of Famer to play for the Giants, Dodgers, and Mets?

The Duke of Flatbush, Edwin "Duke" Snider. Snider debuted with Jackie Robinson in 1947 and the two helped anchor some of the greatest teams in Dodger history. Snider had a home run stroke tailor-made for snug Ebbets Field, and when the team moved west to, initially, play in the Coliseum, his power numbers fell off. In 1962 he collected the first hit in Dodger Stadium and the following year went to the New York Mets. In 1964 he finished his career with the Giants. The popular Snider was elected to the Hall of Fame in 1980.

Numerous players have played for both the Mets and the Yankees, while more than a dozen players have worn the uniforms of the Brooklyn Dodgers, the New York Giants, and the New York Yankees. Only one, however, has done so since 1940—pitcher Sal Maglie.

Who was the last active major leaguer who played for the Brooklyn Dodgers?

Don Drysdale is a good guess, but the answer is Bob Aspromonte. Aspromonte, whose brother Ken played and managed in the major leagues, debuted with Brooklyn at the age of 18, having just graduated from Brooklyn's Lafayette High School. The other teenage Dodger star from Lafayette High? Sandy Koufax. Aspromonte struck out in his one at bat in Brooklyn in 1956, then was brought up to play for the L.A. Dodgers in 1960–61. He played for the expansion Houston team in 1962, and when he left for the Braves in 1969, he was the last Colt 45 to leave the franchise. He retired after the 1971 season, the last active former Brooklyn Dodger.

The last active St. Louis Browns player was Don Larsen, who finished up by pitching four innings for the Cubs in 1967. If Chicago had not signed Larsen, the award for last active Brownie would have gone to Satchel Paige who, in his first big league appearance since 1953, pitched the first three innings against the Red Sox on September 25, 1965. While it was an obvious Charles Finley publicity stunt, Paige allowed just one hit—to Carl Yastrzemski—and no runs.

Most Valuable Players

Roger Maris's record effort in 1961 was rewarded when he was named the American League MVP, winning by just four points over Mickey Mantle, who was injured late in the season. It was Maris's second MVP in a row; he won the year before by just three points over Mantle. Until Barry Bonds and Frank Thomas copped consecutive MVP awards, thus ruining a wonderfully symmetrical baseball question, only nine major league players—one and *only* one at each position—had won consecutive MVPs (known as the Landis Award) since the BBWAA started the modern MVP voting in the 1931 season. Who are the nine players?

Third baseman Mike Schmidt (1980–81), shortstop Ernie Banks (1958–9), second baseman Joe Morgan (1975–76), first baseman Jimmie Foxx (1932–33), catcher Yogi Berra (1954–55), and the tough one, pitcher Hal Newhouser (1944–55). The outfield is in right, Maris (1960–61), in center, Mantle (1956–57) and in left, Dale Murphy (1982–83). The outfield requires some shifting since Murphy was a Gold Glove center fielder for most of his career.

Other players almost making this list include: Roy Campanella, who won three awards but did it in alternating years; Ted Williams, who won in 1946 and finished second by a single point the following year to DiMaggio when one writer did not list Williams at all on his ballot; George Foster, who finished second in

1976 and won the following year; Don Mattingly, who won in 1985 but faded to second the next year behind Clemens; Terry Pendleton, who won in 1991 and finished second the following year; and Cecil Fielder, who finished a close second in both 1990 and 1991.

How did it happen that Babe Ruth won just one Most Valuable Player Award?

Before the 1922 season the American League instituted its AL Trophy to replace the Chalmers Award, which was last handed out in 1914, the year Ruth broke in. One of the stipulations of the Trophy was that it could not be won by a player/manager, of which there were a number in those years, or be awarded more than once to the same player. Babe Ruth missed the first 39 days of the '22 season after he and Bob Meusel were fined and suspended for barnstorming in the off-season. His regular season was also interrupted by three suspensions, one for going into the stands after a heckler, and yet the Babe hit .315 with 35 homers and 99 RBIs in 110 games. Still he received not one vote from the writers. In 1923 the voting was unanimous and Ruth received all 64 points, the highest possible, thus eliminating himself from future consideration.

The American League dropped their Trophy after the 1928 season in part due to criticism that a player could win the award just once. One other reason was the owners' objections that players might use the award to try for a bigger contract the following year, a logic not lost on current players and agents. By the time the BBWAA instituted its version of the MVP in 1931, Ruth was 36 and no longer the dominant player in the game.

Who is the only player to win the MVP while playing for a last place team?

The old line "we could've finished there without him" applies to Andre Dawson, who won the award in 1987 with the Cubs, the last place finishers in the NL East. Dawson led the league in homers with 49, and RBIs with 137. In fact, the only times the MVP was awarded to a player on a second-division team, it has gone to Cubbies. Hank Sauer won it in 1953, and Ernie Banks went back-to-back in 1958 and 1959. The Cubs finished fifth in those years.

The Chalmers Award was the first attempt to award an annual prize, a Chalmers automobile, to the leading player in each league. This was in 1911. The prize was discontinued after the 1914 season, as fans were distracted by the new Federal League and the outbreak of World War I. Since then, how many players have been awarded the MVP and never appeared in the World Series?

Just three players—George Sisler, Hank Sauer, and Ernie Banks.

The American League instituted its league trophy before the 1922 season, and the first winner was St. Louis Browns star George Sisler. Sisler won the award with a .420 average and 105 RBIs. He was named on all eight ballots, and, because the rules stated that no teammates could be named on the same ballot, he shut out teammate Ken Williams who led in RBIs and home runs. Despite the presence of these two sluggers, the Brownies finished a game behind New York, the closest that Sisler would ever come to a World Series.

In the National League the two players with MVP honors who never appeared in the World Series are, not surprisingly, both Cubs. Slow-footed slugger Hank Sauer won the honors in 1952 at the age of 35 or 37 or 39 (depending on which birth date is used), when his Cubs finished fifth. Ernie Banks won back-to-back awards in 1958 and 1959, but failed to lead his team out of the second division.

Since league championship play has been introduced a number of players have taken home MVP Awards, made it to the LCS, and no further. These include Dick Allen in 1972, while with the White Sox, Jeff Burroughs (1974), Rod Carew (1977), Dale Murphy (1982–83), Don Mattingly (1985), and Andre Dawson and George Bell in 1987. All of them played in an LCS, but not a World Series.

A common occurrence in the 1960s was that of teammates finishing 1–2 in the MVP voting. It happened eight times that decade, six times in the AL, with Mantle and Maris doing it in consecutive years. However, in the last 20 years the voting has ended that way four times, and only once in the AL.

Which teammates finished 1–2 in the AL MVP voting, and what year?

In 1983 Cal Ripken and Eddie Murray led the O's to a first-place finish and a World Series victory over the Phillies. They both topped .300 and combined for 60 home runs while each knocked in over 100 runs. Ripken edged out Murray in the voting, the only 1–2 finish for teammates since Vida Blue and Sal Bando in 1971.

In the last 20 years, the National League 1–2 finishers include Joe Morgan and George Foster (Reds, 1976), Kevin Mitchell and Will Clark (Giants, 1989), and Barry Bonds and Bobby Bonilla (Pirates, 1990).

Which Most Valuable Players increased their home run, RBIs, and batting average in the following season but did not win the MVP award again?

This unusual feat has been accomplished three times. The first player to turn the trick was Joe DiMaggio of the Yankees. In 1947, "Joltin' Joe" led the Bronx Bombers to the World Championship with 20 homers, 97 RBIs and a batting average of .315. DiMaggio was MVP despite the fact that Ted Williams of Boston won the Triple Crown. The following season, DiMag batted .320 and led the AL with 39 homers and 155 ribbies. The MVP vote, however, went with Cleveland's player/manager Lou Boudreau, who led the Tribe to a World Series victory over the Boston Braves. Boudreau finished runner-up to Ted Williams in batting with a .355 average, stroked 18 home runs and drove home 106 runs. The latter two marks were both third on the team behind Joe Gordon (32,124) and Ken Keltner (13,119).

Thirteen years later, Frank Robinson powered the Cincinnati Reds to the National League pennant with a .323 BA, 37 home runs, and 124 RBIs. Expansion came to the league the next season, and Robinson feasted. He hit .342, clouted 39 homers, and delivered 136 runs. VP honors, however, went to Los Angeles' Maury Wills, who narrowly missed leading the Dodgers to a pennant. Wills' 104 stolen bases sparked L.A., who finished in a tie with the San Francisco Giants. The Giants went on to win the pennant by defeating the Dodgers in a three-game playoff.

The most recent player to turn the trick was Mo Vaughn of the Boston Red Sox in 1995. Vaughn's .300 average, 39 home runs, and 126 ribbies won him enough votes to secure the AL Most Valuable Player honor. The next year he raised his average 26 points while adding 5 more homers and 17 more RBIs. Juan Gonzalez was named MVP, however, for leading the Rangers to the AL West crown.

Since the MVP award was first given out in 1931, there has only been one other player to increase his totals in all three categories in the following season. That player was Barry Bonds, who was named MVP in both seasons. The Pittsburgh Pirates won the NL East title in 1992 led by Barry Bonds, who batted .311 with 34 homers and 103 runs batted in to take the NL award. The following season saw Bonds move on to the San Francisco Giants, where he hit 46 homers, drove in 123 runs, and batted .336. The Giants failed to win the pennant despite winning 103 games. They finished in second place in the NL West, one game behind the Atlanta Braves.

The Red Sox lost the 1975 World Series to the Cincinnati Reds, a team that won 108 games during the regular season and swept the Pittsburgh Pirates in the NL playoffs. Who were the four MVP award winners (one would win it subsequently) in the Big Red Machine's starting lineup?

The Reds' four MVPs were second baseman Joe Morgan (1975 and 1976), catcher Johnny Bench (1970 and 1972), third baseman Pete Rose (1973), and left fielder George Foster (1977). The 1951 and 1961 Yankees are the only other World Series teams to feature four players who won or would win the MVP: Joe DiMaggio, Mickey Mantle, Phil Rizzuto, and Yogi Berra in 1951; Mickey Mantle, Elston Howard, Yogi Berra, and Roger Maris ten years later.

The team with the *most* MVP winners, past and future, was the 1933 edition of the St. Louis Cardinals, which featured seven: Jim Bottomley, Dizzy Dean, Frankie Frisch, Rogers Hornsby, Joe Medwick, Bob O'Farrell, and Dazzy Vance. Even with all this talent, the Cardinals finished in fifth place.

The World Series Most Valuable Player Award was instituted in 1955 and the first winner was Brooklyn's Johnny Podres. Podres won two games against the Yankees, including a seventh-game shutout, to give the Dodgers their first ever World Championship. Since then, the MVP Award has, with one exception, always gone to a player on the winning team. Who is the lone player to win the MVP Award without winning a ring?

The one player to win it while on a losing team is Bobby Richardson in 1960. The Pirates won the Series, but the Yankees won the battle of statistics, scoring 55 runs to the Pirates' 27, while outhitting the Bucs .338 to .256. Richardson hit .367 and drove in 12 runs to win the award, although it could easily have gone to teammates Whitey Ford, who pitched two shutouts, or Mickey Mantle, who hit .400 with 11 RBIs.

Trades

In 1954 the popular Bobby Thomson was traded to the Braves for Johnny Antonelli, a move that infuriated Giants fans, but the uproar quickly died when Antonelli won 21 games his first season at the Polo Grounds. Antonelli is one of a handful of players debuting after WW II who never appeared in a minor league game but went on to play in the majors at least ten years. Four of these nine are in the Hall of Fame. Who are the others?

Johnny Antonelli, 1948–61
Dick Groat, 1952–67
Ernie Banks, 1953–71 (although he did play in the Negro Leagues), HOF
Al Kaline, 1953–74, HOF
Billy O'Dell, 1954–67
Sandy Koufax, 1955–66, HOF
Catfish Hunter, 1965–79, HOF
Dave Winfield, 1973–95
Bob Horner, 1978–88

What player has been traded the most times?
Depending on how you view it, there are several players who qualify for the frequent flyer award. Bobo Newsom started his career in 1929 with the Brooklyn Dodgers and finished in 1953 with the Philadelphia A's. In between, the 6' 3" right-hander won 211 games, pitched in two World Series and two All-Star Games, three times won 20 games, and four times led in losses. Buck played for nine teams in his career—the Browns, Sena-

tors, Red Sox, Tigers, A's, Cubs, and all three New York teams. Newsom must've kept a bag packed at all times, because he had five separate stints with the Senators, three stays with the Browns and two each with the A's and Dodgers. All told, the Buck was passed, traded, sold, or waived 16 times.

Bob Miller came up with the Cardinals just four years after Newsom left the majors and enjoyed relative stability for the first ten of his 17 years. He went to the Mets in their first season of 1962 and roomed there with the *other* Bob Miller, but after going 1–12 he was sent packing to the Dodgers. In 1968 he went to Minnesota for two years, and from 1970 on he played for seven teams: the Indians, Cubs twice, White Sox, Padres twice, Pirates, Tigers, and back to the Mets again. There were ten different uniforms in Miller's closet when he hung them up for good in 1974.

Who is the only player since WWI to lead his league in home runs after being traded during the season?

Despite tying a White Sox club record in 1950 with 29 home runs, Gus Zernial was traded the following April to Philadelphia in a blockbuster three-way deal. The White Sox got Minnie Minoso in the swap, and the A's welcomed Big Gus, who led the circuit in home runs (33) and RBIs (129) as well as outfield assists (18). Among AL sluggers, only Mickey Mantle, Yogi Berra, and Larry Doby hit more homers in the 1950s than this blonde Texan, who is still the only home run leader traded during the season.

Mark McGwire was traded in August of 1997 from the A's to the National League Cardinals, and while he didn't lead either league in home runs, he led the majors.

In 1915, Braggo Roth hit four homers for the White Sox and then three more after he was swapped to Cleveland. His seven led the league that year, the lowest total ever to lead a league— this is also the number of teams he played for.

Including Mark McGwire, there are nine men who have led the league in home runs with two different teams. But there's only one who lead the league in homers while playing for *three* different teams. Who is the Hall of Famer?

"Mr. October" Reggie Jackson. While with Oakland, Reggie won the title in 1973, 1975, and again with the New York Yankees

141

in 1980 when he shared the crown with 41 homers. Following five tumultuous years in New York, Reggie signed with California in 1982 and again led the AL in homers that year.

The eight men who led the league in homers for two teams are: Cy Williams, who led the NL in 1916 with the Cubs and three more times with the Phillies. The last time, in 1927, when he tied Hack Wilson, Cy did it at the age of 39, the oldest to ever win or share a home run title. Babe Ruth led the league 12 times, the first two with the Red Sox; Jimmie Foxx led the AL three times with the A's and a fourth with the Red Sox; John Mize, twice with the Cardinals and twice with the Giants; Dave Kingman, with the Cubs and Mets; Tony Armas, with Oakland and Boston; Fred McGriff, with the Blue Jays and Padres; and finally Big Mac with Oakland and the Cardinals.

Only one batter has won the batting championship after being traded within his own league in mid-season. Can you name the Moose?

First baseman Dale Alexander hit .343 and .326 his first two years with the Tigers in 1929–30 and led the AL in hits his rookie year. The big first baseman had power as well, hitting 20+ homers each year. His only liability was in the field. His power deserted him in 1931, though he still hit .325. By June 12 of 1932, Alexander was just 4-for-16 and the Tigers sent him to the Red Sox for Earl Webb. Installed as the regular first sacker, Alexander went on a tear, hitting .372 for the remainder of the season to finish at a league-high .367. He went to the plate just 392 times, but he qualified for the title by appearing in more than 100 games (actually 124 games), the rule at the time. The following year, his last, Dale hit a more modest .281 and he and his iron glove were sent packing. He finished his five-year career with a .331 average and the dubious honor of being the only batting champ traded in mid-season.

Willie McGee was traded by the St. Louis Cardinals to Oakland on August 29, 1990, and helped the A's win a pennant, hitting .274. He left behind a .335 average, good enough to win the NL batting title.

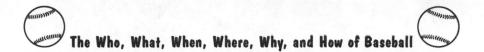
Has any player been traded twice during a season in which he drove home 100 or more runs?

Although it's relatively rare, there have been several players who drove in 100 runs while splitting a season between two teams. Only one time, however, has a player appeared in games for three different teams in a 100-RBI season. In 1998, Mike Piazza began the season with the Los Angeles Dodgers. When it appeared Piazza's asking price for a new contract would be too high, he was traded to the Florida Marlins in a deal many considered the biggest of all time. Piazza's tour of duty with the Marlins didn't last long. Just one week later, Florida sent him packing to the New York Mets in a trade which brought the Marlins several young prospects. Piazza finished out the year with the New Yorkers, almost leading them to a wild card berth in the league playoffs. His record for the year showed a total of 111 runs batted in—30 for Los Angeles, 5 for Florida, and 76 for New York.

Piazza is also the only catcher to notch 200 hits in a season. Mike stroked 201 safeties for the Dodgers in 1997, though only 186 of his hits came while he was catching. The other 15 came as either a pinch-hitter or designated hitter.

Rookies

In 1975 Fred Lynn and Jim Rice formed the most potent rookie tandem in major league history as they both hit over .300 with a combined 43 home runs and 207 RBIs. They finished 1–2 in the AL Rookie of the Year voting that year, and led the Boston Red Sox to the American League pennant. Rice hit .309 with 22 homers and 102 RBIs that year, but it wasn't enough to win Rookie of the Year honors as Lynn hit .331–21–105 and also won a Gold Glove for his play in center field. Lynn is the only player in major league history to be named Rookie of the Year and MVP in the same season (Rice was third in the voting). Who is the only *pitcher* to win the Rookie of the Year and Cy Young Awards in one season?

Fernando Valenzuela. In 1981 Valenzuela led the Los Angeles Dodgers to a World Championship with a 13–7 record and a 2.48 ERA and topped all National League pitchers in innings (192), shutouts (8), and strikeouts (180). He beat out the Expos' Tim Raines for the Rookie of the Year Award and edged the Reds' Tom Seaver for the Cy Young. Doc Gooden in 1984 was the NL Rookie of the Year but finished a distant second to Rick Sutcliffe in the Cy Young Award voting.

Who is the only player to win a batting title his first *two* years in the majors?

Tony Oliva, who is also the only rookie to lead the league in hitting. Along with Dick Allen, Oliva collected more than 200 hits his rookie year of 1964, and his total of 217 set an AL rookie mark. Oliva took the batting title with a .323 average and had a whopping 374 total bases. He led AL hitters the following year with a .321 average, the second of his three batting titles, but ultimately bad knees limited his effectiveness.

Bubbles Hargrave was the NL leader in 1926 with a .353 average, despite going to bat just 336 times. By current rules, top honors would have gone to rookie Paul Waner (.336). With 536 at bats, he was the league's fifth best hitter, but he was only one of the five to go to the plate more than 336 times. One reference book gives the title to Waner, though the rules at the time stated that a player qualified for the title if he appeared in at least 100 games. An exception to this rule was made in 1938 when Jimmie Foxx was given the batting title over Taffy Wright. Wright appeared in 100 games but had just 263 at bats.

In 1941, Pete Reiser's first full season in the majors, he led the NL in hitting and slugging percentage. Many considered him a rookie that year, though he had nearly half a season for Brooklyn the year before. It wasn't until 1957 that "rookie" was given an official definition; the current rule specifies that a player will be considered a rookie unless he's been to bat 130 times, pitched 50 innings or accumulated 45 days or more on the active roster in any previous seasons.

Five players, all American Leaguers, have hit thirty home runs in their first two seasons in the majors. Can you name the quintet?

Rudy York was the first player to accomplish this, hitting 35 four baggers in 1937 and 33 the following season. In his rookie year, York put together one of the most devastating tears ever when he broke Babe Ruth's record for most homers in a month. Rudy hit 18 in August, a record eclipsed by Sammy Sosa in 1998.

Oakland's pair of Jose Canseco, in 1986 and 1987, and Mark McGwire in 1987 and 1988, also topped the 30-homer mark their first two seasons. McGwire obliterated Wally Berger's rookie home run record when he clubbed 49 homers, and both won Rookie of the Year honors.

After hitting 90 homers in two years in the minors, Indiana strong boy Ron Kittle, clubbed 35 homers in 1983, making the All Star Team and winning Rookie of the Year honors with the White Sox. He hit 32 homers in 1984, but his average slipped to

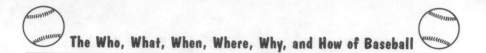

.215. An injury the next year hampered his production and he was dealt to the Yankees following a .213 season in 1986.

Boston's Nomar Garciaparra, another Rookie of the Year, belted more than 30 homers in 1997 and again in 1998, just the fifth player to accomplish this.

Not including rookies, which player had the most hits in his first season with a new team?

Lefty O'Doul first made it to the majors in 1919 as a pitcher with the New York Yankees. Arm trouble caused him to surrender any idea of a career as a hurler, so O'Doul turned to the outfield where he would eventually make his mark as one of the game's all-time great sluggers. Following the 1928 season with the Giants, manager John McGraw traded him to the Phillies in exchange for Freddy Leach. O'Doul prospered in the comfortable confines of Philadelphia's Baker Bowl. He tattooed National League pitching for a league-leading .398 average in 1929, setting a Senior Circuit record with 254 hits in the process. No player has ever had more hits in his first season with a new team. The previous record had been set just the year before by Hall of Famer Heinie Manush. Manush had been traded by Detroit to the St. Louis Browns following a down year in 1927. In 1928, he pounded out 241 hits for his new team, good for a .378 batting average, just one point behind league-leader Goose Goslin. Ironically, Manush and Goslin were the key participants in a trade between St. Louis and Washington in mid-1930. Manush made history of a sort three years later. In Game Four of the 1933 World Series against the Giants, he became the first player ever ejected from a Series contest when he snapped umpire Charley Moran's tie after disagreeing with a Moran call.

Another player who showed immediate dividends in a big way for his new team was Cecil Fielder. Fielder played four years with Toronto in the late 1980s with limited success and then was sold to Hanshin of the Japanese Central League in 1989. Upon his return to the States with the Detroit Tigers in 1990, he proceeded to clout 51 home runs to lead the American League. He also led the circuit in four-baggers the next season, and in runs batted in three consecutive years.

What is the record for most rookies in a lineup?

A full nine. On September 27, 1963, manager Harry Craft of the second-year Houston Colt 45's, penciled in rookies at all nine spots. The lineup included P Jay Dahl, 17; C Jerry Grote, 20; 1B Rusty Staub, 19; 2B Joe Morgan, 20; 3B Glenn Vaughan, 19; SS Sonny Jackson, 19; and outfielders Brock Davis, 19, Aaron Pointer, 21, and Jim Wynn, 21. In his only major league game, Dahl lost 10–3 to the Mets, with rookie Joe Hoerner relieving in his major-league debut. Dahl was killed two year later in an auto accident, at 19, the youngest former major leaguer to ever die.

It was a talented lineup as Joe Morgan went on to play 22 years; Jim Wynn played 15, Jerry Grote played 16, while first sacker Rusty Staub played 23 seasons. Aaron Pointer had his one hit of the year in that game, but his sisters would do even better—they had a top–10 hit of "Fire" by Bruce Springsteen.

What Rookie of the Year played with three major league teams before winning the award?

Lou Piniella. Sweet Lou had his ticket punched by a number of major league teams on his way to winning top rookie honors. He was drafted by the Washington Senators, had a sip of coffee with the Baltimore Orioles in 1964, and made his next appearance with the Cleveland Indians in 1968. Manager Birdie Tebbetts, a former catcher, had plans to put Piniella behind the plate, but in trying to hold on to the fastballs of Sudden Sam McDowell, Lou took so many lumps that he quit catching and was sent back to the minors. He was next drafted by the expansion Seattle Pilots in 1969, and at the end of spring training, he was traded to another expansion team, the Kansas City Royals. It was there, finally, that he became a regular. His .282 the first year was good enough for Rookie of the Year honors.

In the 1950 season opener at Fenway between the Red Sox and Yankees, it looked all over in the fourth inning as Boston's Mel Parnell had a 9–0 lead. Rookie Billy Martin replaced Jerry Coleman in the sixth and in his first big league at bat two innings later he doubled off the Red Sox starter. The Yanks batted around and Martin came up a second time

147

in the inning, this time singling off reliever Al Papai, as New York won the game 15–10. Martin was the first rookie ever to have two hits in an inning in his first game. Who later tied Martin's mark?

White Sox rookie Russ Morman tied Martin's record in 1986. Batting in the fourth inning on August 3 at Comiskey against the Tigers, Morman homered and singled. In his first at bat in the second inning, he smacked a single. Not bad for his first day on the job. Morman went on to play five years for the Sox and Royals.

Who is the only second baseman to win the AL Rookie of the Year Award?

Rod Carew. The Minnesota rookie hit .292 in 1967 to win the award, hit .273 the following year, and followed it with 15 consecutive seasons of .300+ hitting. Carew moved to first base in 1975 to lengthen his career, and two years later won the MVP Award.

Who was the last manager to win the World Series as a rookie?

As a rookie manager in 1961, Ralph Houk led the New York Yankees to a 109–53 record in the regular season and a 4–1 win over the Cincinnati Reds in the World Series. He also led the Yankees to the pennant in 1962 and 1963, but never reached the postseason again in 17 more seasons with New York, Detroit, and Boston.

Tom Browning won 11 straight games for the Reds his first year, the best streak by a Cincy pitcher in 30 years. He won 20 that year, but still finished second to Vince Coleman in the Rookie of the Year voting. Who is the only 20-game winner to be named Rookie of the Year?

Browning's first year total was the highest since 1954 when the Yankees' Bob Grim took Rookie of the Year honors with a 20–6 record. Grim was also the most efficient 20-game winner in history; he is the only one ever to win 20 while pitching fewer than 200 innings. Browning is not the first 20-game winner to be snubbed for top rookie honors; Gene Bearden in 1948, Alex Kellner in 1949, and Harvey Haddix in 1953 all were 20-game winners and all finished second in the voting.

The Dodgers seemingly have always been blessed with talented rookies, starting with Jackie Robinson, who won the first rookie award, through Eric Karros and Mike Piazza. But Big Blue's vein of top rookies was especially rich in one stretch when, for four years in a row, the top honors went to a Dodger player. Who were the four Dodger rookies?

Starting in 1979, four straight National League top rookie awards went to Rick Sutcliffe, Steve Howe, Fernando Valenzuela, and Steve Sax. The pudgy Valenzuela, who set off Fernandomania at Dodger Stadium in his spectacular freshman year, recorded eight shutouts in his 13 wins that year, and was named the Cy Young winner and *The Sporting News* Player of the Year.

Which is the only non-expansion team never to have a Rookie of the Year winner?

Pittsburgh. Since the award was instituted in 1947, the Pirates have never had a top rookie, although there have been Pirate runners-up. Donn Clendenon got the only vote in 1962 that didn't go to the Cubs' Kenny Hubbs, Johnny Ray lost a close vote to Steve Sax in 1982, Al Oliver tied for second behind Ted Sizemore in 1969, Mike Dunne in 1987 was a distant second to Benito Santiago of San Diego, and Orlando Merced placed second behind Jeff Bagwell in 1991.

The year before the official award was instituted, the home run leader was Pittsburgh's Ralph Kiner, generally conceded to be the top rookie. But *The Sporting News* gave the award to the Phillies' Del Ennis. So when it comes to top rookies, everyone has passed the Buc.

Who is the only player to be brought up after the All-Star Game and be named Rookie of the Year?

Willie McCovey. The 1959 Giants had slipped out of first place by late July and were looking for some help to regain the top spot, and they got it in the form of lanky Willie McCovey, who was leading the PCL with a .372 average, 29 homers, and 92 RBIs. Starting against Robin Roberts on July 30, McCovey debuted with four hits, including two triples, the sixth player this century to start with a four-hit bang. Led by McCovey, the Giants won eight of the next nine to go back in first. Though

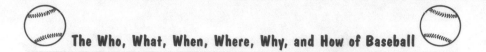

they would just miss the pennant, it was not McCovey's fault. Willie hit .354 in his two months in the big leagues and was the unanimous choice for top rookie in the National League. His 29 homers held up as the most in the PCL that year, so he is the only player to win a minor league home run title, and a major league Rookie of the Year Award—in the same year!

The Draft

Bob Feller was just 17 when he took the mound in 1936, posting a 5–3 record that year. Johnny Antonelli was 18 when he went from high school to the Boston Braves in 1948. David Clyde, the number one pick in the 1973 draft, was pitching a week after his high school graduation, but arm trouble hindered his career. Carl Scheib was just 16 when he relieved for the A's in 1943, while Rogers Hornsby McKee, 16, debuted for the Phils in 1944. Who was the youngest pitcher to throw in the major leagues in this century?

In the 19th century, Fred Chapman was just 14 when he pitched for Philadelphia against Cleveland in a forfeited 9–0 game. It was his only appearance. In this century, the honors go to Joe Nuxhall, who was 15 when he pitched for the Cincinnati Reds in 1944. Even with the players' ranks depleted because of the war, Nuxhall was pounded for five runs in his one inning. He didn't return to the majors until 1952 but did become a solid performer for the Reds.

Jim Derrington was two months shy of his 17th birthday when he started for the White Sox in the last game of the 1956 season. He lost to Kansas City, but is still the youngest pitcher to start a game this century.

Who was the last player to go directly from high school to the major leagues?

Mike Morgan was 18 when Charlie Finley signed him for the A's in 1978, two days after Morgan's graduation from high school. Morgan, the fourth overall draft pick, threw a complete

game in his debut, a 3–0 loss to the Orioles' Scott McGregor. After going 0–3, Morgan was mercifully sent to the minors where he bounced around the Yankees, Mariners, and Orioles organizations. He finally became a solid starter with the Dodgers at the age of 29, and later, in his 20th season, served up number 62 to Mark McGwire in 1998.

The other high school first-round choice of Finley's in 1978 was Tim Conroy, who made the leap with Morgan to the A's. Conroy pitched in two games before going to the minors for more seasoning. Four years later he was back up with the A's and pitched six more years in the majors before shoulder problems slowed his 95-mph fastball. No team has duplicated Finley's publicity stunt since then, and no high school grad has bypassed the minors and/or college baseball.

One A's pitcher of the 1930s later signed his son to the same team, and after inking the contract Junior pitched the following week. Who are the pair?

Lew Krausse Junior and Senior. Senior compiled a 5–1 record in two years with the A's, then in Philadelphia, but his most notable game was a non-decision against the Indians on July 10, 1932. To save money on the A's single game appearance in Cleveland, owner/manager Connie Mack brought along just two pitchers, Krausse and Eddie Rommel. Krausse started and was gone after one inning and four hits. Rommel then relieved and gave up a record 29 hits in 17 innings of relief, but won when the A's took it 18–17! As an A's scout in 1961, Krausse signed his son for a $125,000 bonus, and a few days later Lew Jr. started for Kansas City and matched his father's farewell game by throwing a shutout, a 4–0 win over the Angels. After 12 games he went to the minors but returned to compile a 14–9 record in 1966.

Besides giving up 29 hits—including a major league record nine to Johnny Burnett—in a winning cause, Ed Rommel set a mark of another sort. Which innovation did he pioneer?

He was the first umpire to wear glasses. Rommel is considered the father of the modern knuckleball, and he used it to lead the league in wins in 1922 and 1925. He retired as a player after the 1932 season with 171 victories, then returned to the majors in 1938 as an umpire. He umped for 22 years and, on Opening Day of 1956 at Griffith Stadium, appeared on the field wearing spectacles. That day Mickey Mantle hoisted two prodigious homers out of the capacious park, one landing on a house and the other hitting a clump of trees.

Who was drafted by four professional teams when he graduated from college?

Big Dave Winfield was a 13–1 pitcher who hit over .400 for the University of Minnesota, and was named the 1973 College World Series MVP. A starter on the Golden Gophers basketball team, Winfield was drafted by the NBA Atlanta Hawks and the ABA Utah Stars, and, despite never having played football, the NFL Minnesota Vikings drafted him in the 17th round. Picked fourth overall by San Diego, Winfield signed with the Padres.

One player was a college All-American for two years and was the first player selected in the 1978 draft. He went directly to the majors, the last time a first pick in the draft made that jump. As a Braves starter, he hit a home run in his first game. Who was the star?

Bob Horner. The first player selected in the 1978 draft, Horner played ten years in the majors, interrupted by one year in Japan with the Yakult Swallows. Two years earlier, the top pick had been another Arizona State player, Floyd Bannister.

The number one pick in the June draft of high school and college players is the most sought-after baseball prospect in the land. Sports agents salivate at the thought of representing this blue chipper, who is a sure shot to make the majors. In fact, only one number one pick since the draft began in 1965, has failed to do so. Who was it?

In the 1966 June draft the New York Mets passed up the chance to select Reggie Jackson, a flamboyant sophomore outfielder for Arizona State, who then signed with the A's. The Mets went for high school catcher Steve Chilcott from Lancaster, California, who signed for a $75,000 bonus. Chilcott labored for six years in the minors before being released, the only first pick never to make the majors. The Mets did come out a winner that year, however, when they won the rights to sign a young pitcher from California, Tom Seaver. Seaver had been drafted in the January phase by Atlanta, but the Braves signed him after he started pitching for USC, and the contract was voided.

Alas, it appears that the number one pick in the 1991 draft will join Chilcott as the other first pick not to make it. The Yankees selected Brien Taylor ahead of Arizona State's Mike Kelly, and the promising left-hander hurt his arm in a bar room brawl. He is still struggling in the minors to regain his form.

Only one player has been selected as the top pick *twice* in the June draft. Who was this sought-after player?

Danny Goodwin. While other first-round picks that year included Frank Tanana, Jim Rice, and Rick Rhoden (the prizes were in the second round: Mike Schmidt and George Brett), the White Sox spent the top choice in 1971 on Goodwin, a high school catcher from nearby Peoria. Goodwin turned down a reported $50,000 signing bonus to attend Southern University. Four years later, Goodwin was again the top pick, this time by the Angels. He played briefly for California and two other teams before being shunted off to the minors, and a decade later he was out of baseball—after twice being the most sought-after player in America.

While a majority of first-round picks make it to the major leagues, it is certainly not true of picks from the later rounds. But, happily, it does happen. For example, Colorado's Mark Brownson, a 30th round pick in 1993, pitched a shutout over the Astros in his 1998 major-league debut. One player, who was selected *last* in the entire draft, went on to become a star. Who was it?

As a favor to Dodger manager Tom Lasorda, Los Angeles selected his godson with the last pick on the 62nd round of the 1988 draft, taking a young first baseman/catcher from Dade County Community College, Mike Piazza. Much earlier they had used the draft's fifth pick to take their first choice, pitcher Bill Benes. Piazza did not blossom until 1992 when he hit .300 for the first time in the minors, and the Dodgers called him up at

the end of the year. Since then he has been a perennial All-Star. Benes, meanwhile, never did control his 95-mph fastball and never made the majors.

Stadiums

What was the first ballpark to be called a stadium?

Yankee Stadium. Before the Yankees built the stadium, which opened in 1923, ball fields reflected the pastoral beginnings of baseball, and all of them had names like park or field or grounds. The new structure was named a stadium to show its urban, rather than rural, setting. The Yankees had two homes before moving to their present address, Hilltop Park (or American League Park, as it was often called) and the Polo Grounds, which they shared with the Giants.

Hall of Fame pitcher Don Drysdale began his career in Brooklyn in 1956 and pitched 14 years in the Dodger blue. He won a league-high 25 games in 1962, but the sidearmer's greatest achievement probably came in 1968, the year of the pitcher. He reeled off six consecutive shutouts on the way to a record 58 consecutive shutout innings, a mark since broken by Orel Hershiser. Drysdale threw 49 shutouts in his illustrious career to tie for 21st on the all-time list. His first shutout came in a home game. Where was it?

No, not Brooklyn or Los Angeles. Jersey City. The Dodgers played seven games in New Jersey in 1956, eight in 1957, and starting in 1958 they made the complete move west, to Los Angeles. Taking the mound at Roosevelt Field on June 5, 1957, Drysdale faced the Cubs and threw his first shutout, winning 4–0. He was also the losing pitcher in the last game at Roosevelt Field, a 3–2, 12-inning loss to the Phillies.

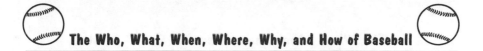

Which is the only stadium in the past 50 years to be home to both an American League champion and an NL winner?

Milwaukee's County Stadium was the home field of the 1957 Braves when they won the championship and home to the Brewers in 1982 when they took the AL East. The Brewers went on to beat California then lost to the Cardinals in seven games.

Before that, the last park to host both league winners was Sportsman's Park in St. Louis, which was the home field for both the Browns and the Cardinals. In 1944 the Browns won their only AL pennant and then lost to the Cardinals in the Series.

Sticklers might point out that Shea Stadium was the home field of the Mets and, briefly, the Yankees, who were tenants in 1974–5 while Yankee Stadium was being rebuilt, thus qualifying as an answer. But the Bombers waited till they were back in the Bronx in 1976 before they captured another AL pennant.

Which major league team had *two* home parks at the same time?

An evasive and cute answer might include the Angels, who occupied Chavez Ravine while their new stadium was being built, or the Yankees at Shea during the remodeling of Yankee Stadium. Or even the Dodgers, who crossed the Hudson to play a few games in Jersey City, just before going to Los Angeles.

But the answer is the Indians who called both Municipal Stadium and League Park their home fields. League Park, built in 1891, was initially the home of the National League Cleveland Spiders, the worst team in history. From 1901 on it was home to Cleveland's American League team. League Park, with a seating of some 21,000, was cozy and intimate, though the dimensions in left (375 ft.) and center (420 ft.) were roomy enough. Right field was just 290 feet down the line and it was here that Ruth hit his 500th home run.

When Municipal Stadium was completed in an unsuccessful attempt to lure the 1932 Olympics to Cleveland, the Indians moved in and played 77 games there in 1933. But the weekday crowds seemed lost in the giant structure, and the following year the Tribe went back to League Park for those games. For the larger weekend crowds, Municipal Stadium was the home field. This two-stadium practice continued from 1933 until 1946, when League Park deteriorated to a point of no return. In 1945 temporary stands there collapsed during a Cleveland Rams NFL game, and the next year the team moved to comparatively safer quarters in Los Angeles.

The site of Super Bowl 26 (or XXVI for those who took Latin) in 1992 when Washington beat Buffalo 37–24 was one of just three stadiums to host a Super Bowl *and* a World Series. Which stadium was it, and what were the other two?

Minnesota Metrodome is the answer. This stadium was finished in time for the 1982 baseball season, and the much-criticized ballpark has proved to be a great home field advantage. The thickest pad in the majors makes fly balls that land a real adventure, and the loudest stadium in the majors seems to disconcert visiting teams. In 1987 and again in 1991, the host Twins won a World Series in seven games by losing every road game and winning all four matches at home.

A second site was San Diego's Jack Murphy Stadium, named after the writer-brother of the Mets' announcer Bob Murphy, which hosted the 22nd Super Bowl in 1988 when Washington ripped Denver, 42–10. The Padres hosted both the 1984 World Series with the Tigers and the 1998 World Series with the Yankees.

The last stadium was the Los Angeles Coliseum, site of Super Bowl I between Green Bay and Kansas City in 1967, and site of the seventh Super Bowl when Miami beat Washington, 14–7, in 1973. While Chavez Ravine was under construction, the Dodgers played the 1959 World Series at the Coliseum and won it in six games. Game Five, which Sandy Koufax lost 1–0, drew a record crowd of 92,706.

Which stadium has been the site of the most home runs in a season?

The answer is Wrigley Field—Los Angeles' Wrigley Field, also named for the chewing gum magnate. When the American League awarded a franchise to Gene Autry after the 1960 season, the new owner went looking for a site for the expansion Angels. The Dodgers were still playing in the Los Angeles Coliseum while their new stadium at Chavez Ravine was under construction, which left Wrigley Field, the former PCL stadium, as the only other wheel in town. The park was owned by the Dodgers, who had traded their Ft. Worth franchise to the Cubs for it plus the L.A. franchise when the team moved from Brooklyn. Knowing they would be playing in a 20,000 seat park with 345 foot power alleys, the Angels drafted some beef like Steve Bilko, Ted Kluszewski, and Leon Wagner, all of whom helped the Angels hit 122 homers at home that year; they hit just 67 on the road. Daddy Wags led with 28 home runs, 19 coming at home.

The bad news was that their opponents hit 126 in the friendly confines for a record 248 dingers. Baltimore's Jim Gentile led the visitors with eight of his 46 homers that year coming at Wrigley. Of Maris's 61 homers in 1961, just two were hit in L.A. Even with all the fireworks, the team failed to pull 20,000 fans for any game, and the next year they became tenants in spacious Chavez Ravine.

The 1974 Sacramento entry in the PCL was stocked with future Brewers like Gorman Thomas and Sixto Lezcano and the Solons took advantage of the intimate dimensions of their home park to hit an organized ball record 305 home runs that season.

What player holds the season record for hitting the most home runs at home?

No, it's not Roger Maris who hit just 30 at Yankee Stadium in 1961, or Babe Ruth who powered 28 at home in 1927 (he did hit 32, his best, at the Stadium in 1921), or Mark McGwire, or Sammy Sosa. In 1998, Sammy Sosa hit 35 homers at Wrigley Field, while down the river Mark McGwire pounded out 38 homers at home, second on the all-time list.

Topping the sluggers is Hank Greenberg, who hit 58 home runs for the Tigers in 1938 and collected 39 of them at the newly rebuilt and renamed Briggs Stadium. That same season, Jimmie Foxx collected 35 of his 50 home runs at Fenway. Just behind them come Ted Kluszewski, who hit 34 of his 49 at Crosley Field in 1954, followed by Hack Wilson in 1930, with 33 at Wrigley and 23 on the road.

The top sluggers who disliked road food were Ralph Kiner, in 1948, with 31 of his 40 dingers coming at Forbes Field, and the

St. Louis Browns' Ken Williams, who in 1922 collected 32 homers at Sportsman's Park and just seven while traveling. New York Giant Mel Ott hit all 18 of his 1943 homers at his home Polo Grounds en route to a career total of 323 there, the most by any one player at any one park. And Gavvy Cravath hit all of his league-leading 19 homers at Philadelphia's Baker Bowl in 1914.

What player, besides Ruth and Maris, has hit the most home runs in a season on the road?

If you read the previous answer carefully, you calculated that Maris hit 31 on the road in 1961 and Ruth must've hit 32 while traveling. In fact, the House that Ruth Built was not the Babe's favorite park. Not by a long shot. In a *New York Sun* interview in May 1927 Ruth remarked, "All the parks are good except the Stadium. There is no background there at all. But the best of them is the Polo Grounds. Boy, how I used to sock 'em there. I cried when they took me out of the Polo Grounds."

In 1998, Mark McGwire belted 32 road homers to tie the Babe for most homers away from home. Ruth never had to hit in Cincinnati's Riverfront Stadium, where George Foster hit just 21 of his 52 home runs in 1977. Foster is tied for third on the list of road sluggers with 31 that year. In 1998 Sammy Sosa hit 31 homers away from Wrigley, and Brady Anderson hit 31 of his 50 homers in 1996 on the road. Mickey Mantle (30 of his 54) and Baltimore's Jim Gentile (30 of 46), both in 1961, and Eddie Mathews (30 of 47 in 1953, the first year at Milwaukee County Stadium) complete the list of sluggers with 30 or more home runs on the road.

On the topic of road homers, the 1945 Washington Senators found their home park of Griffith Stadium a particularly tough place in which to hit 'em out. The team hit 26 four-baggers on the road, but just one at home—an inside-the-park homer by Joe Kuhel!

Forbes Field was home to a National League team for over 60 years before being abandoned in 1970 for a new multipurpose stadium across town. Fans never saw a no-hitter at Forbes Field, and it was host to the World Series just four times. The finest moment at Forbes came in Game Seven of the 1960 World Series, when the Pirates beat the New York Yankees

10–9. The victory came on a game-winning home run in the bottom of the ninth inning—the first time a World Series ended on a home run. Which Pirate delivered that historic blow?

Second baseman Bill Mazeroski. Leading off the bottom of the ninth, Mazeroski homered off New York's Ralph Terry to give Pittsburgh a 10–9 win and its first World Championship since 1925. The Pirates won the Series despite being outscored 55 runs to 27.

Toronto's Joe Carter hit a Game Six home run off Mitch Williams in the 1993 World Series to end the Series and the career of "the Wild Thing." Philadelphia fans were so down on Williams after the gopher ball that he was dealt to Houston over the winter. After a rocky start in 1994, Williams was released.

On May 25, 1935, a future Hall of Famer hit the last three home runs of his career at Forbes Field, including the first ball ever to clear the right field roof. Who was this star?

Babe Ruth. After being released by the Yankees, Ruth played 28 games for the Boston Braves in 1935. He batted just .181, however, and retired in early June.

When right-handed slugger Hank Greenberg was sold to the Pirates before the 1947 season, the bullpens at Forbes Field were moved to left field and the shortened distances became known as "Greenberg Gardens" in anticipation of the many home runs that would surely land there. Instead, one of Greenberg's teammates led the NL with 51 home runs that year, part of a record seven consecutive seasons in which he led the league in homers. Who was the slugger?

Ralph Kiner. Kiner led the NL in home runs each year from 1946 to 1952, including a career-high 54 in 1949. Greenberg retired after the 1947 season, and "Greenberg Gardens" became "Kiner's Korner" instead.

Chicago's Wrigley Field was the last to have lights, the switch being turned on August 8, 1988. But the stadium might have been lit up as early as 1942. The lights had been purchased by owner Phillip K. Wrigley and only the advent of WW II stayed the order to install them. Instead, Wrigley donated the lights

to a naval yard where shipbuilding was going on 24 hours a day. After the war the Cubs were the only National League team without lights and Wrigley decided to leave it that way. Which American League stadium was the last to be electrified?

Detroit's Briggs Stadium in 1948. The stadium was first constructed in 1900 and called Bennett Field, named after a popular 19th century Detroit player who lost his legs in a train accident. The stadium seated just 8,500. The park was enlarged a number of times, first in 1912, when it was renamed Navin Field, and finally in 1937, when construction made the field look very much like today's stadium.

Brooklyn's Ebbets Field opened for play in 1913 and closed for major league baseball when the Dodgers moved west. In between it hosted some memorable and raucous times both on the field and in the stands. The right field wall was plastered with ads such as clothier Abe Stark's "Hit this sign and win a free suit of clothes," while a sign in earlier years proclaimed "Zack Wheat caught 400 flies last season, Tanglefoot fly paper caught ten million."

Night baseball came to Ebbets Field on June 15, 1938, when the Dodgers turned the lights on for the first time. A crowd of 38,748 crammed in that night, while 15,000 were turned away, and many fights broke out in the stands because of duplicate seat assignments. On the field the pregame ceremony featured an appearance by Babe Ruth and a race between Olympic sprinter Jesse Owens and Dodger speedster Ernie Koy. Koy, whose son Ernie, Jr. later played for the NFL Giants, beat Owens with the help of a 10-yard head start. But Koy was wearing his baseball flannels while Owens had track shorts.

What else happened that night?

Cincinnati pitcher Johnny Vander Meer threw his second straight no-hitter. The 23-year-old Vandy had beaten Boston on June 11 in Cincinnati 3–0 to set the stage for the memorable game. Vander Meer walked seven Dodgers, including three in the ninth inning, but held on to win 6–0. In his next start, Vandy gave up a hit in the fourth to end a streak of 21 hitless innings, an NL record.

Stars and Stripes

When did the custom begin of the playing of the National Anthem at games?

During the seventh-inning stretch of the 1918 World Series opener, a military band played "The Star Spangled Banner," though it was not yet adopted as the National Anthem. From then on, it was played at every World Series game and season opener, and whenever a band was present, though "America the Beautiful" opened one of the games in the 1998 World Series. The custom of playing the song before every game began during WW II when the installation of public address systems made it feasible.

The 1918 World Series is also remembered for starting in early September, the leagues cutting the season short because of WW I. To limit the use of trains, the first three games were played in Chicago, with the next three in Boston. The Cubs moved their home games to Comiskey Park to take advantage of the larger seating capacity, but only 19,000 fans showed up for the September 5 Series opener when Red Sox lefty Babe Ruth dueled Hippo Vaughn. Ruth prevailed 1–0 en route to his consecutive scoreless innings streak of 29.

The popular version of the seventh-inning stretch is that it was inadvertently created by a United States President who was attending a Pirates game in Pittsburgh after the turn of the century. As the story goes, the President was in need of a stretch and stood up in the middle of the seventh inning. The crowd, thinking he was leaving the stadium, respectfully

stood up. There are accounts that go back to the 1860s of crowds standing up and stretching, so it seems that he might not have been the one to start this time-honored custom. But there is one practice that he did start, that of throwing out the first pitch of the season. Who is this chief executive?

William Howard Taft. The 300-pound Taft started the custom on April 14, 1910, when he tossed out the first ball at the opener in Washington. It was caught by Walter Johnson, who then entertained the President by hurling a one-hit shutout, giving up an easy fly hit that fell into the overflow crowd which had spilled onto the field for a ground-rule double.

Three weeks later in St. Louis, Taft showed that he was a baseball fan by attending a Reds-Cardinals game at Robison Field. When the Cardinals walked to a big lead (Reds pitchers walked 16 batters in that May 4 game), Taft exited for Sportsman's Park to watch the Browns tie Washington 3–3 in 14 innings.

While Taft was the first president to throw out a ball at an opener, he was not the first president to attend a major league game. That honor *officially* goes to Benjamin Harrison, who watched Washington lose 7–4 to the Reds on June 6, 1892, though Andrew Johnson reportedly viewed a game in August 1865 between Washington and the Philadelphia A's. In April of 1892, Ohio governor William McKinley was at an Opening Day game between Toledo and Columbus, but McKinley never attended a major league game after he became president.

Other presidents made it out to the ballpark as well. Woodrow Wilson would occasionally watch a game at Griffith Stadium from his limousine, and during Prohibition, President Hoover was greeted at the 1929 World Series in Philadelphia by fans chanting "We want beer."

Which president played in the college World Series?

George Bush. Bush was a light-hitting first baseman for Yale in 1947 when the Eli went to the college World Series. The Yale team was captained by the future president, but the star of the team was a right-handed pitcher named Frank Quinn. Quinn signed a $50,000 bonus with the Boston Red Sox, appeared in a few games, but never had a major league decision.

Several presidents were fine football players, including Dwight Eisenhower and Gerald Ford. But Eisenhower once remarked, "Not making the baseball team at West Point was one of the greatest disappointments of my life, maybe the greatest."

Hall of Fame

What regular-season game featured the most Hall of Famers in one lineup?

The 1927 Yankees, arguably the greatest team in history, had six future Hall of Famers among their players, while the Yankees of 1928 upped that total to nine (Ruth, Gehrig, Lazzeri, Combs, Hoyt, Durocher, Pennock, Dickey, and Coveleski). The 1933 Cardinals had eight, and other teams with seven future Hall of Famers include the 1927 and 1929 Giants, the 1934 Pirates, and the 1927 and 1928 Athletics. Each of the 1930–33 Yankee teams had nine Hall of Famers on the roster at some time during the season. But only once has it happened that one team had seven Hall of Famers in a game at the same time.

It was the Philadelphia Athletics who fielded this group on June 11, 1927, and only in the ninth inning. The outfield consisted of Ty Cobb in right, Al Simmons in center and Zack Wheat in left. Jimmie Foxx played first with Eddie Collins at second, and Lefty Grove pitching in relief. Cy Perkins was catching and batting seventh but when Mickey Cochrane pinch-hit for him in the last inning there was, briefly, a lineup of seven future Hall of Famers.

The most in two lineups occurred the next year when, on May 24, a record 13 future Hall of Famers took the field as the Yankees played the A's. This number didn't include nonplaying Hall of Famers Herb Pennock and Stan Coveleski, managers Miller Huggins and Connie Mack, or umpires Tom Connally and Bill McGowan. The 13 in the lineup included Combs, Durocher,

Ruth, Gehrig, Lazzeri, and Hoyt for New York; Cobb, Speaker, Cochrane, Simmons, Collins, Grove, and Foxx for the A's.

What Hall of Famer was thrown out of a major league baseball game without ever appearing in one?

Basketball great Bill Sharman.

It happened on September 27, 1951. The Dodgers were playing the Braves but had their eyes on the advancing Giants, the team that would eventually win the pennant on Thomson's dramatic "shot heard 'round the world." On the Dodger bench was young Bill Sharman, brought up after hitting .286 at Ft. Worth. With the score tied 3–3 in the eighth, umpire Frank Dascoli called Braves outfielder Bob Addis safe on a play at the plate, and the Dodgers erupted in protest. Dascoli ejected several players before gesturing that the whole bench, Sharman included, was also "outa da game." Sharman played the next year at St. Paul before giving up hardball for the hard wood. He set a number of free throw records on his way to the Basketball Hall of Fame, but remains the only player ejected from a major league baseball game without ever appearing in one.

What three Hall of Famers hit home runs in their first major league at bats?

Earl Averill, the holder of six career records for the Indians, hit a home run in his first at bat on Opening Day, 1929. He was the second American Leaguer to ever accomplish the feat, following Luke Street.

The next AL player to homer his first time up also became a Hall of Famer—Ace Parker, who was elected to *football's* Hall of Fame in 1972. Parker's roundtripper was a pinch homer—the first ever in a first at bat in the AL—for the A's in 1937, and then he hung up his baseball spikes (and his career batting average of .179) the following year to concentrate on football. He was the NFL's MVP in 1940.

The last Hall of Famer to do it was Hoyt Wilhelm, the knuckleballing relief pitcher brought up by the New York Giants in 1952 at the advanced age of 28. Wilhelm posted a 15–3 record that year and led the league in ERA. He hit a home run in his first at bat, and it turned out to be the only roundtripper of his long career.

Frank Robinson was one of the premier players of the 1950s and 1960s. He broke in with the Reds in 1956, made the All-Star Team, and smashed 38 homers to tie Wally Berger's rookie record. In 1961 he won the NL MVP Award when he led Cincinnati to its first pennant since 1940. After a 1965 season in which Robby hit .296 with 33 homers and 113 RBIs, GM Bill DeWitt, declaring Frank "an old 30," traded the intense competitor to Baltimore. Robinson responded by winning the AL Triple Crown and the MVP Award when he led the Orioles to the pennant in 1966. Robinson led the O's to another pennant in 1969 when he hit .308 along with 32 homers and 100 RBIs, the fifth time he reached .300+, 30+ homers, and 100 RBIs in a season. Only 16 players have reached that plateau four times and all but one of the eligible names have made it to the Hall of Fame. In this group, what former teammate of Frank Robinson's is the only one *not* in Cooperstown?

Ted Kluszewski. Big Klu, he of the cutoff sleeves and awesome power, is the only player to hit .300 with 30 homers and 100 RBIs, do it four times, and not make the Hall. Even players such as Rogers Hornsby, Mickey Mantle, and Al Simmons have reached it only three times. Kluszewski was a good, if not far-ranging, first sacker, and he led the NL five straight times in fielding, but it was with his bat that the former Indiana football star was feared. Kluszewski had three straight years where he had *40+* homers, with 100 RBIs and a 300+ average; only six other players—Babe Ruth, Lou Gehrig, Jimmie Foxx, Willie Mays, Hank Greenberg, and Duke Snider—have accomplished that three or more times.

Frank Robinson was a fierce performer who excelled in every facet of the game. He was a Gold Glove outfielder and a stolen base percentage leader, and he set an NL rookie record when he was hit 20 times with pitches. Who is the only player to get hit 50 times in a season by pitches?

The black and blue award goes to Ron Hunt who got plunked 50 times while playing for Montreal in 1971. Only Hugh

Jennings with the old Baltimore Orioles in 1896 is close with 49. When Hunt retired his liniment, he had led the league in that category seven years and been hit 243 times. Subsequently, Don Baylor retired with the major league mark—in more ways than one—of getting hit by pitches 267 times.

Frank Robinson and Cal Ripken, Sr. share a record together. What is it?

The two were the Oriole managers during their record 21-game losing streak to start the 1988 season. Robinson coached and managed various teams before returning to Baltimore as a coach in 1985. The Orioles got off to a poor start in 1988, losing their first six games, and Robinson replaced Ripken as the manager. Together the two managed 21 straight losses before Mark Williamson and Dave Schmidt combined to beat the White Sox 9–0. The previous worst start by a team was 0–13.

What all-time great played 21 years with the same American League team, racking up several records that are still untopped? One of the marks was hitting .433 in 1925. After retiring as a player, he wore the same team's uniform as manager for four years before moving on to Cleveland to manage the Indians.

Walter Johnson. He was a good-hitting pitcher throughout his career, and for one year, a great-hitting pitcher. At the age of 37, he hit .433, still the highest mark for a hurler, while winning 20 games for the Nats. In all, The Big Train won 417 games for the Washington Senators, the most wins by a pitcher for one team. Only Cy Young won more games in his career than Johnson, and he did it for five teams.

Walter Johnson was one of just five original players to be voted into baseball's Hall of Fame in that first class of 1936. Who were the others?

Joining Johnson in that first magnificent class of inductees were Babe Ruth, Ty Cobb, Honus Wagner, and Christy Mathewson. By the time the building was officially opened in Cooperstown in 1939, the original five had been joined by the likes of Grover Cleveland Alexander, Nap Lajoie, George Sisler, Eddie Collins, Tris Speaker, Cy Young, Connie Mack, and others.

Walter Johnson is among the top ten in a number of pitching categories, but in one major category he is the all-time leader. Which one?

Shutouts. The Big Train threw 110 shutouts in his career, and 38 of those shutouts were 1–0 squeakers. The next man on the list of 1–0 wins is Grover Cleveland Alexander with 17. Johnson needed to throw shutouts with the weak-hitting Senators supporting him; the team was below the league batting average in 15 of Johnson's 21 years on the mound.

Johnson also lost a record 20 1–0 games, one of them in 11 innings on August 28, 1913, to end his 14-game winning streak, and three others in 1916–17 while matched against pitcher Babe Ruth. Another came on September 17, 1916, at the hands of future Hall of Famer George Sisler, Sisler's last victory as a pitcher before he concentrated on first base.

Who is the only foreign player in the Japanese Hall of Fame?

The one foreigner is not a hurler who mowed down batters at Dodger Stadium or a slugger who poled home runs into the Yankee Stadium bleachers, but rather a Russian pitcher named Victor Starfin.

Following the Bolshevik Revolution, Konstantin Starfin, his wife, and young son Victor left Russia, eventually settling in the small city of Asahikawa, on the island of Hokkaido in 1925. Young Victor was an exceptional athlete and by 1934 had grown into an outstanding high school pitcher. At 6' 4" he towered over the Japanese of the 1930s, and his fastball was overpowering. When Yumiuri formed Japan's first professional team, Starfin was recruited to pitch, and in 1937, the year that Japan's professional league began, he won 28 games, compiling a 1.70 ERA.

Except for 1945, Japanese baseball continued through the various Japanese military conflicts and WW II, even though many of the able-bodied were in the armed forces. Because he was not Japanese, Starfin was exempted from the military, but his numbers were exceptional by any standards. In 1939 he won 42 games while posting an incredible ERA of 1.01. All this in a 96-game schedule! The following year he racked up 38 wins. When his career ended in 1955 he had won 303 games and was the first 300-game winner in Japanese baseball. Starfin was struck

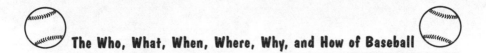
and killed by a car two years later while crossing a street and today is the only foreigner in the Japanese Baseball Hall of Fame at Korakuen Stadium in Tokyo.

Note that we said foreigner, for baseball purists will know that legendary slugger Sadaharu Oh is also not Japanese. Oh is Chinese but was born in Tokyo to a Chinese father and retains his citizenship as a matter of pride. He too is in the Hall of Fame.

Uniforms

Which team was the first to wear numbers?

The first team to wear numbers was the Cleveland Indians, who started a game on June 26, 1916, with players wearing paper numbers pinned to their sleeves. The numbers corresponded to the player's position on the lineup card—the leadoff batter getting number 1 and the pitcher pinning on number 9. This was fine as long as players didn't move around in the order from day to day, but the experiment was soon abandoned.

It was not until Opening Day of 1929 that the Yankees appeared on the field with permanent numbers and they too assigned numbers according to a player's position in the lineup. The Yanks handed out uniforms number 1 through Arandt Jorgen's number 32, skipping number 13 and number 23. Babe Ruth, batting third, received number 3, and Lou Gehrig, as the cleanup hitter, got number 4. By 1931 all the American League teams had numbered uniforms, and by 1933 the National League had followed suit.

Bill Veeck, in 1960, was the first to put names on the backs of uniforms when he labeled his Chicago White Sox players. Ted Turner got even cuter with the Braves in the mid-70s when he put nicknames on the backs of the uniforms. Thus, Darrell Chaney became "Nort" (after Art Carney's character in "The Honeymooners") and Rogelio Moret was "Gallo." He also tried assigning the nickname "Channel" to pitcher Andy Messersmith, who wore the number 17; Turner's cable network, WTBS, just happened to be on channel 17. But the fashion experiment was not copied by other teams and it soon went the way of Chief Nokahoma.

The number of years in the same uniform is a mark of longevity, loyalty, and ability. Walter Johnson pitched 21 years for Washington but got into fewer than 1,000 games. Since 1900 only eight players have played 2,500 games without ever changing team uniforms. All but three are in the Hall of Fame, and the exceptions played in the 1990s. Can you name this group?

The active player is of course Cal Ripken, Jr. A good argument can be made that, with the advent of free agency, this list won't change in the future. For now, the list of players, all of whom played at least part of their career after WW II, includes:

Ernie Banks, Chicago Cubs (1953–71)	2,528
George Brett, Kansas City Royals (1973–93)	2,707
Al Kaline, Detroit Tigers (1953–74)	2,834
Stan Musial, St. Louis Cardinals (1941–44, 1946–63)	3,026
Mel Ott, New York Giants (1926–47)	2,730
Brooks Robinson, Baltimore Orioles (1955–77)	2,896
Carl Yastrzemski, Boston Red Sox (1961–83)	3,308
Robin Yount, Milwaukee Brewers (1974–93)	2,856

Who was the first player to have his number retired?

Lou Gehrig. On July 4, 1939, in one of the most famous ceremonies in baseball history, a tearful Gehrig announced his retirement from baseball. Before 61,808 fans at Yankee Stadium, he said, "Today, I consider myself the luckiest man on the face of the earth." After his speech, Babe Ruth grabbed Gehrig in a bear hug, and Columbia Lou's pinstriped number 4 would be later retired, making him the first player so honored. He died less than two years later of ALS (amyotrophic lateral sclerosis), now called Lou Gehrig's disease.

What pitcher won just nine games and still had his number retired?

Jim Umbricht. The 33-year-old journeyman had pitched five years in the majors when he died of cancer in April 1964. The expansion Colt 45's picked up the reliever from the Pirates and he was 8–1 in relief for Houston, 9–5 for his career. The untimely death of Umbricht, who had performed well for the new team,

173

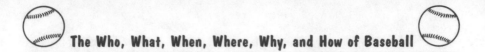

and the need of the Colts to be like the older teams and retire a number, resulted in the action.

Houston also retired the number of another pitcher who died before his time. Hard-throwing Don Wilson won 104 games for the Astros between 1966 and 1974, including two no-hitters. In a September 1974 game, with the Astros behind 2–1 to the Reds, he was lifted after eight innings despite having allowed no hits. Wilson committed suicide the following January and he became the second Houston player to have his uniform number retired.

Who is the only Washington Senator to have his number retired?

The only Washington Senator number ever retired was not that of the immortal Walter Johnson, but the number 47 of infielder Sherry Robertson, the first Canadian player to have his number retired. Huh, you say? Robertson, a .230 hitter who played for the Nats between 1940 and 1951, just happened to be the nephew of owner Clark Griffith. Robertson's number was never "officially" retired, just permanently taken out of commission. Harmon Killebrew, who started his career with the Senators and then went with the team to Minnesota, had his number 3 retired, but it was as a Twins player.

Odds and Ends

The year 1939 saw several innovations and noteworthy events in baseball. Ted Williams debuted, the Hall of Fame was dedicated and opened in June, and Lou Gehrig retired. The year also saw the first telecast of a baseball game. Which teams were involved and where?

The great experiment took place at Columbia University's Baker Field on May 17, 1939. A single camera covered the action, the figures were diminutive and the picture fuzzy, and fewer than 400 sets were in use to receive the picture relayed from the top of the Empire State Building. No future major leaguers were in the collegiate lineups when Princeton topped Columbia 2–1 in ten innings of the first game of a doubleheader. However, all-time college and pro quarterback Sid Luckman was in the Lions' lineup. The announcer who risked the seeing eye of the camera was Bill Stern. As a football announcer he covered gaffes in his play-by-play by improvising phantom laterals to get the ball into the hands of the correct ball carrier. The following day, in a review of the broadcast, the *New York Times* sniffed, "It is difficult to see how this sort of thing can catch the public fancy."

The first telecast of a major league game occurred a few months later on August 26, 1939, at Ebbets Field, when Red Barber announced a doubleheader between the Dodgers and Cincinnati Reds over W2XBS. Red also worked in the first commercial between innings. Years later, when he became a New York Yankees broadcaster, he had the TV camera pan the nearly empty Yankee Stadium. The real story, drawled the

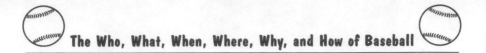

fearless redhead, was that the House that Ruth Built was housing fewer than 1,000 fans soured by a losing team. The Yankees were not amused and fired the broadcaster for his candid reporting.

Red Barber, along with Connie Desmond, also announced the first game ever telecast in color. This occurred on August 11, 1951, a doubleheader between the Dodgers and Boston Braves. The Dodgers won the first game 8–1 and stretched their lead the National League to 13½ games, a seemingly insurmountable lead. But the Giants win the pennant, the Giants win the pennant.

With games going well over three hours these days, it is refreshing to remember that at one time they were routinely under two hours. When did the shortest game in the major leagues take place?

The record was set in 1919 when a game between the Giants and the Phillies took just 51 minutes to complete, with the Giants winning 6–1. It was the last day of the season and undoubtedly the Phils just wanted to get the whole thing over with. They finished 47½ games out that year.

The next shortest game was in the AL on September 26, 1926, when the Browns zipped by the Yankees in just 55 minutes in the second game of a doubleheader. The Brownies swept the two games in a total time of two hours and seven minutes. It was the last game of the season, the Yankees having clinched the pennant the day before by sweeping the Browns. In the season finale, Ruth hit homer number 47, but the highlight was Browns' coach Jimmie Austin, 46, knocking in a run with a double and then stealing home.

The shortest game *ever* played in organized baseball was 1913, and, yes, the month was September. A Southern Association game between Mobile and Atlanta took just 32 minutes to complete when players on both teams agreed to swing at every good pitch and little time was taken between pitches. There were no strikeouts and one walk as Mobile won, 2–1.

What is the longest game on record?

This could be answered in several ways—innings or minutes. Or even the time between when a game is suspended and when it is completed. The longest AL game on record was in 1984 between the Brewers and the White Sox, when Harold Baines's 25th-inning homer ended the marathon 7–6. The game, suspended on May 8 after 17 innings, was finished before the regular game on May 9. Tom Seaver pitched the final inning to pick up the victory then won the regularly scheduled game as well. Time of the game was a record eight hours and six minutes.

By contrast, a 26-inning duel between the Braves and the Dodgers on May 1, 1920, took just three hours and 30 minutes. Joe Oeschger shut out Brooklyn in the last 21 innings and was matched by Leon Cadore, who went 20 scoreless innings. The majors' longest game ended in a 1–1 tie. The next day, the Dodgers lost in 13 innings to the Phils, then returned to Boston to lose in 19 innings. Three days work resulted in 58 innings and two losses.

The longest game *ever* in organized ball was started on April 19, 1981, and finished June 23. The score was 2–2 after 32 innings between Pawtucket and Rochester (International League) when the players staggered off the field at 4:07 A.M. The suspended match resumed two months later, and Pawtucket scored in bottom of the 33rd to give Bob Ojeda the win. Wade Boggs and Cal Ripken combined to go 6–25 in the game, which took eight hours and 25 minutes to complete.

The desire to drop a baseball from great heights was probably the same one that prompted ballplayers (and others) to drop water bombs from hotel windows. Who caught the first ball dropped from a newsworthy height?

Despite a carefully contrived claim by Gabby Street that he was the first to do this when he stood at the foot of the Washington Monument on August 21, 1908, and held on to a dropped ball, the honors go to Pop Shriver. Shriver, playing for Cap Anson's Chicago White Stockings, caught a ball from that same monument 14 years earlier, on August 24, 1894. Clark Griffith, a Chicago pitcher at the time, dropped the ball for Shriver. When Street's claim was publicized, the earlier catch was never mentioned, thus helping the survival of one of the most enduring false legends of baseball.

Which Hall of Famer holds the record for catching a ball dropping from the greatest height?

Gabby Hartnett shared in this madness by risking injury on April Fool's Day 1930 in Los Angeles, where the Cubs were to play their Angels farm club in a preseason match. Before the game a blimp flew at 800 feet above L.A.'s Wrigley Field and a ball was tossed out. Hartnett watched the ball descend and grabbed it, then caught the next toss for good measure.

Which player caught something other than a baseball from a great height?

Wilbert Robinson was gulled into accepting a challenge to catch a baseball dropped from an aeroplane flying over the Brooklyn Dodgers' spring training site in 1914. But aviatrix Ruth Law forgot to take along a baseball and instead substituted a small grapefruit. It plummeted down and splashed into the glove of a surprised Uncle Robbie, knocking him down, but he held on to complete the fruitful outing. In a later embellishment, Casey Stengel was named the culprit. Not so. Casey, a member of the team, was not yet in camp.

Ed Delahanty was the premier 19th-century slugger and one of five brothers to play major league baseball. He narrowly missed the Triple Crown in 1893, led the NL in hitting in 1899 with a .410, and topped the AL in hitting in 1902. How did his career end the following year?

Delahanty and the Senators parted company in July of 1903 when he jumped the team after being benched due to conditioning. Delahanty left the club in Detroit and took a train across Canada to New York, but at International Bridge near Niagara Falls, a conductor threw the drunk and disorderly Delahanty off the train. Attempting to walk across the bridge in the dark, he fell (or jumped, or was pushed) to his death.

Delahanty was not the first, nor would he be the last, major leaguer to die during a season. Delahanty debuted with the Phils in 1888, just three weeks after the team's star pitcher, 25-year-old Charlie Ferguson, died of typhoid fever. Ferguson

had four 20-game seasons. **What major leaguers have died as a result of an injury sustained on the field?**

The first death attributed to play was that of Jim Creighton, the premier player of his day. In October 1862, Creighton had four doubles in a game but suffered a ruptured bladder hitting a home run. He died four days later. In the 1909 season opener, Athletics catcher Doc Powers ran into a wall while chasing a foul pop up and suffered internal injuries. Despite three operations for "intestinal problems," he died two weeks later.

But the most dramatic fatal injury occurred on August 16, 1920, when the Yankees' submariner Carl Mays wheeled an inside pitch on Indians shortstop Ray Chapman, who was crowding the plate. Instead of ducking away, the veteran Chapman froze and the pitch struck him in the head. He died the next day. Despite abuse by players and fans, Mays continued to throw well and the following year led the league in wins, percentage, and innings pitched. Mays ended his career with a 2.92 ERA, and a winning percentage of .623, better marks than two other Yankee pitchers of his era—Herb Pennock and Waite Hoyt, both of whom are in Cooperstown.

Several minor leaguers have died from on-field injuries, including one incident that occurred four years earlier than the Chapman beaning. Former major leaguer Johnny Dodge, playing for Mobile in the Southern Association in 1916, was hit in the face by a pitch and died as a result.

What major leaguer committed suicide during the season?

Only one player, Willard Hershberger, a catcher with the Reds in 1940. Filling in for the injured Ernie Lombardi, Hershberger was hitting .309 when he committed suicide in a Boston hotel room on August 3. Hershberger, who had been despondent for weeks, blamed himself for calling the wrong pitches in a 5–4 loss to New York three days earlier. Pitcher Bucky Walters retired the first two Giant batters in the ninth inning, and had two strikes on each of the next four hitters, but Harry Danning and Burgess Whitehead each hit a homer with a man on. The night before his death, Hershberger talked for two hours with Reds manager Bill McKechnie and told him, "My father took his own life, and so will I." The Reds retired his uniform number 5,

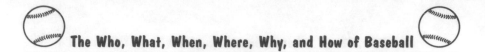

but reinstated it two years later. They would later retire it again in honor of another Cincinnati catcher, Johnny Bench.

One other suicide was that of Boston outfielder Chick Stahl, who was named manager after the 1906 season. In spring training the following March, he returned to his room after breakfast and killed himself by drinking three ounces of carbolic acid. Stahl left a note saying, "Boys, I just couldn't help it. It drove me to it." He might have been right; the guilt-ridden team finished in seventh place in the American League.

Another victim of mid-season suicide was Harry Pulliam, who was elected the president of the National League in 1903. Pulliam was instrumental in forging the peace between the older NL and the upstart AL, but, suffering from mental illness, he took a leave of absence in February 1909. He returned to work during the season, but on July 29, 1909, he committed suicide.

What hitter once struck the same fan twice with foul balls?

This is such an oddity that we had to throw it in. Richie Ashburn, the long-time center fielder for the Phillies, was renowned for his ability to foul off pitch after pitch until he got one that he liked. Records aren't kept about foul balls hit, but one incident did make it into print. It happened in a home game on August 17, 1957, against the Giants. Ashburn hit a line drive into the box seats behind third base and the ball struck a spectator named Alice Roth and broke her nose. Alice's husband Earl Roth was sports editor of the *Philadelphia Bulletin*. The game was briefly stopped while Ms. Roth was being administered to. The game commenced and Ashburn's next foul again hit Ms. Roth as she was being carried out on a stretcher.

Who was the first major leaguer to play baseball in the Japanese Leagues?

The answer is two players, Leo Kiely and Phil Paine, both doing it in 1953 while they were in the army and stationed in Japan. Paine started with the Braves in Boston in 1951 and rejoined them in Milwaukee in 1954. He finished with the Cards in 1958 with a nifty 10–1 career mark. In nine games with the Nishitetsu Lions in 1953, he won four, lost three, and sported a 1.77 ERA.

Kiely was 7–7 in a half season with the Red Sox in 1951 before entering the military. In 1953 he went 6–0 in six games for the Mainichi Orions. He came back to the Red Sox in 1954, was sent to the bullpen, and saved 12 games for the Sox in 1958, two years before he retired.

The first American traded to a Japanese team was Clete Boyer. In 1971 after his major league career was over, Boyer was playing for Hawaii (PCL) when he was traded to the Tayio Whales for John Werhas.

When were colored balls first introduced?

Charlie Finley, the colorful and combative owner, attempted a number of innovations during his stormy years as head of the A's. One suggestion for speeding up the game was having three balls equal a walk. Tried in 1971 during an exhibition game with the Brewers, the pitchers combined for 19 walks, and the idea was dropped. For the same reason, 19th-century baseball pioneer Harry Wright once suggested that the umpire hide the ball and strike count from the batter. This suggestion was never adopted either.

Finley pushed for the use of orange baseballs, contending that they were easier for a batter to spot, but even fellow rebel Bill Veeck scoffed at the idea. "My dad thought about that in the '20s when male fans all wore white shirts. How many wear white shirts these days?" Finley's idea never made it out of spring training.

But the notion of colored balls was put into effect back in the 1930s by executive Larry MacPhail, the man who introduced commercial airline flying and, in 1935, night baseball to the major leagues. Three years later, while with the Dodgers, MacPhail had official baseballs dyed dandelion yellow for an August game with the Cardinals. The Dodgers won 6–2, though the Cards Johnny Mize hit a Fred Fitzsimmons' knuckler for the first "yellow" home run. The Dodgers used the "stitched lemons" for three more games in 1939 then dropped the idea.

Who was the Baby Ruth candy bar named after?

When the Baby Ruth was introduced by the Curtis Candy Company, they contended that the candy bar was named not for the slugger but for Grover Cleveland's daughter, Ruth, who was born in 1891 and died of diphtheria 12 years later. A cynic might suspect that this was a way out of paying royalties since the candy bar reached the market in 1920, 16 years after the death of the president's daughter but just months after the Babe's second season of leading the majors in homers.

Ty Cobb had a candy bar produced by the Benjamin Candy Company of Detroit, but it's not known whether the candy's lack of success was due to its flavor or Cobb's sourness. Curtis Candy introduced the Reggie Bar in 1978, named after Reggie Jackson, and the candy made another appearance in 1993 to coincide with Mr. October's induction into the Hall of Fame. The Pete Rose Supercharg'r Energy Bar came out briefly in 1980, and the Ken Griffey, Jr. Ice Cream Bar made an appearance a decade later. Even minor leaguers got into the act when the Ducky Wucky Candy Bar was produced in 1932. It was named after the Houston star Ducky Medwick, who hit .354 that year on his way to the Cardinals.

Who was Bill Veeck's midget and how many times did he appear on a major league field?

Eddie Gaedel. Twice. But that's the short answer to one of the most famous incidents in baseball. It was 1951 and Bill Veeck, one of baseball's great promoters, was general manager of the lowly St. Louis Browns, still three years away from sprouting Oriole wings and moving to Baltimore. The Browns were last in the league's standing and attendance, their usual spots, and Veeck was looking for anything to generate interest in the team.

So on August 19, 1951, Veeck unveiled one of his greatest promotions, pinch hitter Eddie Gaedel, a 43-inch midget. Expecting resistance from the umpires, Veeck armed manager Zack Wilson with a legitimate major league contract for Gaedel and, after some discussion, the little slugger was allowed to pinchhit for center fielder Frank Saucier. The first pitch from Detroit's Bob Cain was, not surprisingly, high, as were the next three. Gaedel tossed his bat away, strode to first, and Jim Delsing went in as a pinch runner. Gaedel walked to the dugout and into baseball history. Furious league officials then decreed that all contracts must first go through the league office.

But it was not Eddie's final appearance on the diamond. Bill Veeck moved on to the White Sox and on May 26, 1959, the same day that Harvey Haddix pitched perfect ball against the Braves for 12 innings, Gaedel made another appearance. And this time he brought reinforcements. Before a Cleveland-White Sox game, a helicopter landed behind second base and, led by Gaedel, four midgets dressed as spacemen jumped out. Brandishing ray guns, the four then "captured" 5' 9" Nellie Fox and 5' 10" Luis Aparicio. Gaedel reportedly said, "I don't want to be taken to your leader. I already know him."

Two years later, when the 36-year-old Gaedel died of a heart attack following a mugging in Chicago, his death was virtually ignored by organized baseball. The only major leaguer to attend his funeral was the man he faced, pitcher Bob Cain.

Index of Names

Illustrations
Identified

Nap Lajoie

Rogers Hornsby

Rube Marquard

Babe Ruth

Ty Cobb

Grover Alexander

Cy Young

Mel Ott

Christy Mathewson

Henry Aaron

Warren Spahn

Yogi Berra

Ted Williams

Joe DiMaggio

Sandy Koufax

Stan Musial

Mickey Mantle

Brooks Robinson

Bob Gibson

Willie Mays